IDIOT'S DELIGHT

BY ROBERT EMMET SHERWOOD

IDIOT'S DELIGHT

THE PETRIFIED FOREST

REUNION IN VIENNA

THIS IS NEW YORK

THE VIRTUOUS KNIGHT

WATERLOO BRIDGE

THE QUEEN'S HUSBAND

THE ROAD TO ROME

CHARLES SCRIBNER'S SONS

IDIOT'S DELIGHT

BY

ROBERT EMMET SHERWOOD

CHARLES SCRIBNER'S SONS · NEW YORK
CHARLES SCRIBNER'S SONS · LTD · LONDON
1936

THIS PLAY
IS LOVINGLY DEDICATED TO

LYNN FONTANNE
AND
ALFRED LUNT

IDIOT'S DELIGHT

Presented by the Theatre Guild, at the National Theatre, Washington, D. C., March 9th, 1936, with the following cast:

DUMPTSY	George Meader
ORCHESTRA LEADER	Stephen Sandes
DONALD NAVADEL	Barry Thompson
PITTALUGA	S. Thomas Gomez
AUGUSTE	Edgar Barrier
CAPTAIN LOCICERO	Edward Raquello
DR. WALDERSEE	Sydney Greenstreet
MR. CHERRY	Bretaigne Windust
MRS. CHERRY	Jean Macintyre
HARRY VAN	Alfred Lunt
SHIRLEY	Jacqueline Paige
BEULAH	Connie Crowell
BEBE	Ruth Timmons
FRANCINE	Etna Ross
ELAINE	Marjorie Baglin
EDNA	Frances Foley
MAJOR	George Greenberg
FIRST OFFICER	Alan Hewitt
SECOND OFFICER	Winston Ross
THIRD OFFICER	Gilmore Bush
FOURTH OFFICER	Tomasso Tittoni
QUILLERY	Richard Whorf
SIGNOR ROSSI	Le Roi Operti
SIGNORA ROSSI	Ernestine de Becker
MAID	Una Val
ACHILLE WEBER	Francis Compton
IRENE	Lynn Fontanne

The scene of the play, designed by Lee Simonson, is the cocktail lounge in the Hotel Monte Gabriele, in the Italian Alps, near the frontiers of Switzerland and Austria.

ACT I

Afternoon of a winter day in any imminent year.

ACT II

ACT III

The following afternoon.

IDIOT'S DELIGHT

ACT I

IDIOT'S DELIGHT

ACT I

The cocktail lounge of the Hotel Monte Gabriele.

The hotel is a small one, which would like to consider itself a first-class resort. It was originally an Austrian sanatorium. Its Italian management has refurnished it and added this cocktail lounge and a few modern bedrooms with baths, in the hope that some day Monte Gabriele may become a rival for St. Moritz. So far, this is still a hope. Although the weather is fine, the supply of winter sports enthusiasts at Monte Gabriele is negligible, and the hotel is relying for its trade upon those itinerants who, because of the current political situation, are desirous of leaving Italy.

Near at hand are a railway line into Switzerland, highways into Switzerland and Austria, and an Italian army airport.

At the left, up-stage, is a large doorway, leading to the lobby, in which we can just see the Reception Desk.

At the upper right is a staircase. A few steps up is a landing, above which is a high window with a fine view of the Alpine scenery to the North and

West. The panes are fringed with frost. From the landing, the stairs continue up to a gallery which leads to bedrooms off to the upper left.

Downstairs left is a swinging door marked with the word "BAR."

Over this bar entrance are crossed skis and the head of a mountain goat. On the wall at the right is a Fascist emblem with crossed Italian flags. About the Reception Desk, off to the left, are signs assuring the guest that this hotel has been approved by all the automobile associations of Europe and that Travellers' Cheques may be cashed here. Somewhere on the walls are pictures of the Coliseum and the S.S. "Conte di Savoia."

There are small tables and chairs about, with perhaps a couch or two. At the left is a piano, and when the first curtain rises a dismal little four-piece orchestra is playing "June in January."

Note a line in the dialogue along toward the end of Act One: there is something about this place that suggests "a vague kind of horror." This is nothing definite, or identifiable, or even, immediately, apparent. Just an intimation.

Behind the Reception Desk, PITTALUGA *is occasionally visible. He is the proprietor of the hotel —a fussy, worried little Italian in the conventional morning coat and striped pants.*

On the landing at the upper right, looking dole-

fully out the window, is DONALD NAVADEL, *a rather precious, youngish American, suitably costumed for winter sports by Saks Fifth Avenue. Experienced in the resort business, he was imported this year to organize sporting and social life at Monte Gabriele with a view to making it a Mecca for American tourists. He is not pleased with the way things have turned out.*

DUMPTSY *comes in from the left. He is an humble, gentle little bell-boy, aged about forty, born in this district when it was part of Austria, but now a subject of the Fascist Empire. He has come in to clean the ash-trays. He listens to the music.*

DUMPTSY

Come si chiama questa musica che suonate?

ORCHESTRA LEADER

Il pezzo si chiama: "Giugno in Gennaio."

DUMPTSY

Oh, com'e bello! Mi piace! (*To* DON.) It's good.

DON

Will you please for God's sake stop playing that same damned tiresome thing?

DUMPTSY

You don't like it, Mr. Navadel?

DON

I'm so sick of it, I could scream!

DUMPTSY

I like it. To me, it's good.

DON

Go on, and clean the ash-trays.

DUMPTSY

But they're not dirty, sir. Because there's nobody using them.

DON

There's no need to remind me of *that!* Do as you're told!

DUMPTSY

If you please, sir. (*He whistles the tune and goes out.*)

DON (*to the* LEADER)

You've played enough. Get out!

LEADER

But it is not yet three o'clock.

DON

Never mind what time it is. There's nobody here to listen to you, is there? You can just save the wear and tear on your harpsichord and go grab yourselves a smoke.

LEADER

Very good, Mr. Navadel. (*To the other musicians*) E inutile continuare a suonare. La gente non ascolta più. Si potrà invece far quattro chiacchiere e fumare una sigaretta.

(*They put away instruments and music and start to go out, as* PITTALUGA *appears bristling.*)

PITTALUGA (*to* LEADER)

Eh, professori? Perchè avete cessato di suonare? Non sono ancora le tre.

LEADER

Il Signor Navadel ci ha detta di andare a fumare egli ne ha avuto abbastanza della nostra musica.

(*The* MUSICIANS *have gone.*)

PITTALUGA (*going to* DON)

You told my orchestra it would stop?

DON (*untroubled*)

I did.

PITTALUGA

My orders to them are they play in here until three o'clock. Why do you take it to yourself to countermand my orders?

DON

Because their performance was just a little too macabre to be bearable.

PITTALUGA

So! You have made yourself the manager of this hotel, have you? You give orders to the musicians. Next you will be giving orders to me—and to the guests themselves, I have no doubt. . . .

Don

The guests! (*He laughs drily.*) That's really very funny. Consult your room chart, my dear Signor Pittaluga, and let me know how many guests there are that I can give orders to. The number when last I counted . . .

Pittaluga

And you stop being insolent, you—animale fetente. I pay you my money, when I am plunging myself into bankruptcy. . . .

Don

Yes, yes, Signor—we know all about that. You pay me your money. And you have a right to know that I'm fed to the teeth with this little pension that you euphemistically call a high-grade resort hotel. Indeed, I'm fed to the teeth with you personally.

Pittaluga (*in a much friendlier tone*)

Ah! So you wish to leave us! I'm very sorry, my dear Donald. We shall miss you.

Don

My contract expires on March the first. I shall bear it until then.

Pittaluga

You insult me by saying you are fed with me, but you go on taking my money?

Don

Yes!

Pittaluga

Pezzo mascalzone farabutto prepotente cana-
glia . . .

Don

And it will do you no good to call me names **in**
your native tongue. I've had a conspicuously
successful career in this business, all the way from
Santa Barbara to St. Moritz. And you lured me
away from a superb job . . .

Pittaluga (*as* Don *continues*)

Lazzarone, briccone, bestione. Perdio.

Don

. . . with your glowing descriptions of this
handsome place, and the crowds of sportlovers,
gay, mad, desperately chic, who were flocking here
from London, Paris, New York. . . .

Pittaluga

Did *I* know what was going to happen? Am *I*
the king of Europe?

Don

You are the proprietor of this obscure tavern.
You're presumably responsible for the fact that
it's a deadly, boring dump!

Pittaluga

Yes! And I engaged you because I thought you

had friends—rich friends—and they would come here after you instead of St. Moritz, and Muerren, and Chamonix. And where are your friends? What am I paying you for? To countermand my orders and tell me you are fed . . . (*Wails from warning sirens are heard from off-stage right.* PITTALUGA *stops short. Both listen.*) Che cosa succede?

DON

That's from down on the flying field.

PITTALUGA

It is the warning for the air raids!

(AUGUSTE, *the barman, is heard in bar off-stage, left.*)

AUGUSTE'S VOICE

Che cosa?

(PITTALUGA *and* DON *rush to the window.*)

PITTALUGA

Segnali d'incursione. La guerra e incominiciata e il nemico viene.

(*Airplane motors are heard off right.*)

DON (*looking through window*)

Look! The planes are taking off. They're the little ones—the combat planes.

(CAPTAIN LOCICERO *enters from the lobby. He is the officer in charge of the frontier station. He is tired, quiet, nice.* AUGUSTE *enters from the bar.* DUMPSTY *follows the* CAPTAIN.)

AUGUSTE

Signor Capitano!

CAPTAIN

Buona sera!

(AUGUSTE *helps him take off his coat.*)

DUMPSTY

Che cosa succede, Signor Capitano? È la guerra?

CAPTAIN

No—no—datemi cognac.

(DUMPSTY *puts coat on chair right of table and goes up and exits through arch center.* CAPTAIN *sits chair left of table.*)

AUGUSTE (*as he goes out*)

Si, signor Capitano.

(*The* CAPTAIN *sits down at a table.* PITTALUGA *and* DON *cross to him.* DUMPSTY *goes.*)

PITTALUGA

Che cosa significano quei terribili segnali? È, forse, il nemico che arriva?

DON

What's happened, Captain? Is there an air raid? Has the war started?

CAPTAIN (*smiling*)

Who knows? But there is no raid. (*The porter's hand-bell in the lobby is heard.*) They're only testing the sirens, to see how fast the combat planes can go into action. You understand—it's like life-boat drill on a ship.

(DUMPSTY *enters.*)

DUMPSTY

Scusi, padrone. Due Inglesi arrivati. (*He hurries out.*)

PITTALUGA

Scusi. Vengo subito. Presto, presto! (*He goes.*)

CAPTAIN

Have a drink, Mr. Navadel?

DON

Thank you very much—but some guests are actually arriving. I must go and be very affable. (*He goes.* DR. WALDERSEE *appears on the gallery above and comes down the stairs as* AUGUSTE *enters from the bar and serves the* CAPTAIN *with brandy and soda. The* DOCTOR *is an elderly, stout, crotchetty, sad German.*)

CAPTAIN

Good afternoon, Doctor. Have a drink?

DOCTOR

Thank you very much—no. What is all that aeroplanes?

(AUGUSTE *goes.*)

CAPTAIN

This is a crucial spot, Dr. Waldersee. We must be prepared for visits from the enemy.

DOCTOR

Enemy, eh? And who is that?

CAPTAIN

I don't quite know, yet. The map of Europe supplies us with a wide choice of opponents. I suppose, in due time, our government will announce its selection—and we shall know just whom we are to shoot at.

DOCTOR

Nonsense! Obscene nonsense!

CAPTAIN

Yes—yes. But the taste for obscenity is incurable, isn't it?

DOCTOR

When will you let me go into Switzerland?

CAPTAIN

Again I am powerless to answer you. My orders are that no one for the time being shall cross the frontiers, either into Switzerland or Austria.

DOCTOR

And when will this "time being" end?

CAPTAIN

When Rome makes its decision between friend and foe.

DOCTOR

I am a German subject. I am not your foe.

CAPTAIN

I am sure of that, Dr. Waldersee. The two great
Fascist states stand together, against the world.

DOCTOR (*passionately*)

Fascism has nothing to do with it! I am a scientist. I am a servant of the whole damn stupid human race. (*He crosses toward the* CAPTAIN.) If
you delay me any longer here, my experiments will
be ruined. Can't you appreciate that? I must get
my rats at once to the laboratory in Zurich, or all
my months and years of research will have gone
for nothing.

(DON *enters, followed by* MR. *and* MRS. CHERRY
—*a pleasant young English couple in the first flush
of their honeymoon.*)

DON

This is our cocktail lounge. There is the American bar. We have a thé dansant here every afternoon at 4:30—supper dancing in the evening.

CHERRY

Charming.

DON

All this part of the hotel is new. Your rooms
are up there. (*He crosses to the window.*) I think
you'll concede that the view from here is unparal-
leled. We can look into four countries. (*The*
CHERRYS *follow him to the window.*) Here in the
foreground, of course, is Italy. This was formerly

Austrian territory, transferred by the treaty of
Versailles. It's called Monte Gabriele in honor
of D'Annunzio, Italian poet and patriot. Off there
is Switzerland and there is Austria. And far off,
you can just see the tip of a mountain peak that
is in the Bavarian Tyrol. Rather gorgeous, isn't
it?

CHERRY

Yes.

MRS. CHERRY

Darling—*look* at that sky!

CHERRY

I say, it *is* rather good.

DON

Do you go in for winter sports, Mrs. Cherry?

MRS. CHERRY

Oh, yes—I—we're very keen on them.

DON

Splendid! We have everything here.

CHERRY

I've usually gone to Kitzbuhel.
(PITTALUGA *and* DUMPSTY *appear up-stage and
speak in Italian through the dialogue.*)

PITTALUGA

Dumptsy, il bagaglio è stato portato su?

DUMPSTY

Si, signore, è già sopra.

PITTALUGA

Sta bene, vattene.

DON

It's lovely there, too.

CHERRY

But I hear it has become much too crowded there now. I—my wife and I hoped it would be quieter here.

DON

Well—at the moment—it is rather quiet here.

PITTALUGA (*coming down*)

Your luggage has been sent up, Signor. Would you care to see your room now?

CHERRY

Yes. Thank you.

PITTALUGA

If you will have the goodness to step this way. (*He goes up the stairs.*) 'Scuse me.

CHERRY (*pauses at the window on the way up*)

What's that big bare patch down there?

DON (*casually*)

Oh, that's the airport. (PITTALUGA *coughs disscreetly.*) We have a great deal of flying here.

PITTALUGA

Right this way, please.

CHERRY

Oh—I see. (*They continue on up, preceded by* PITTALUGA.)

DON

And do come down for the thé dansant.

MRS. CHERRY

We should love to.

PITTALUGA

Right straight ahead, please. (*They exit through gallery.*)

DON (*standing on first step*)

Honeymooners.

CAPTAIN

Yes—poor creatures.

DON

They wanted quiet.

DOCTOR (*rises*)

Ach Gott! When will you know when I can cross into Switzerland?

CAPTAIN

The instant that word comes through from Rome. (*The hand-bell is heard.*) You understand that I am only an obscure frontier official. And

here in Italy, as in your own Germany, authority
is centralized.

DOCTOR

But you can send a telegram to Rome, explaining the urgency of my position.

(DUMPSTY *appears, greatly excited.*)

DUMPSTY

More guests from the bus, Mr. Navadel. Seven
of them! (*He goes.*)

DON

Good God! (*He goes out.*)

DOCTOR

Ach, es gibt kein Ruhe hier.

CAPTAIN

I assure you, Dr. Waldersee, I shall do all in
my power.

DOCTOR

They must be made to understand that time is
of vital importance.

CAPTAIN

Yes, I know.

DOCTOR

I have no equipment here to examine them properly—no assistant for the constant observation
that is essential if my experiments are to succeed . . .

CAPTAIN (*a trifle wearily*)

I'm so sorry . . .

DOCTOR

Yes! You say you are so sorry. But what do you *do?* You have no comprehension of what is at stake. You are a soldier and indifferent to death. You say you are sorry, but it is nothing to you that hundreds of thousands, *millions,* are dying from a disease that it is within my power to cure!

CAPTAIN

Again, I assure you, Dr. Waldersee, that I . . .

DON'S VOICE

Our Mr. Pittaluga will be down in a moment. In the meantime, perhaps you and the—the others . . . (*He comes in, followed by* HARRY VAN, *a wan, thoughtful, lonely American vaudevillian promoter, press agent, book-agent, crooner, hoofer, barker or shill, who has undertaken all sorts of jobs in his time, all of them capitalizing his powers of salesmanship, and none of them entirely honest. He wears a snappy, belted, polo coat and a brown felt hat with brim turned down on all sides*) . . . would care to sit here in the cocktail lounge. We have a thé dansant here at 4:30 . . . supper dancing in the evening . . .

HARRY

Do you run this hotel?

Don

I'm the Social Manager.

Harry

What?

Don

The Social Manager.

Harry

Oh! American, aren't you?

Don

I am. Santa Barbara's my home, and Donald Navadel is my name.

Harry

Happy to know you. My name's Harry Van. (*They shake hands.*)

Don

Glad to have you here, Mr. Van. Are you— staying with us long?

Doctor (*rising*)

I shall myself send a telegram to Rome, to the German Embassy.

Captain

They might well be able to expedite matters. (*The* Doctor *goes.*)

Harry

I've got to get over that border. When I came in on the train from Fiume, they told me the border is closed, and the train is stuck here for to-night and maybe longer. I asked them why, but they either didn't know or they refused to divulge their secrets to me. What seems to be the trouble?

Don

Perhaps Captain Locicero can help you. He's the commander of Italian Headquarters here. This is Mr. Van, Captain.

Captain (*rising*)

Mr. Van, my compliments.

Harry

And mine to you, Captain. We're trying to get to Geneva.

Captain

You have an American passport?

Harry

I have. Several of them. (*He reaches in his pocket and takes out seven passports, bound together with elastic. He fans them like a deck of cards and hands them to the* Captain.)

Captain

You have your family with you?

Harry

Well—it isn't exactly a family. (*He goes to the right.*) Come in here, girls!

SHIRLEY (*from off-stage*)

Come on in, kids. Harry wants us.

(*Six blonde chorus girls come in. They are named:* SHIRLEY, BEULAH, BEBE, FRANCINE, EDNA *and* ELAINE. *Of these,* SHIRLEY *is the principal, a frank, knowing fan dancer.* BEULAH *is a bubble dancer, and therefore ethereal.* BEBE *is a hard, harsh little number who shimmies.* DON *doesn't know quite how to take this surprising troupe, but the* CAPTAIN *is impressed, favorably.*)

HARRY

Allow me to introduce the girls, Captain. We call them "Les Blondes." We've been playing the Balkan circuit—Budapest, Bucharest, Sofia, Belgrade, and Zagreb. (*He turns to* DON.) Back home, that would be the equivalent of "Pan Time." (*He laughs nervously, to indicate that the foregoing was a gag.*)

CAPTAIN (*bowing*)

How do you do?

HARRY

The Captain is head man, girls.

GIRLS

How do you do? . . . Pleased to meet you. . . . Etc.

HARRY

The situation in brief is this, Captain. We've got very attractive bookings at a night spot in

Geneva. Undoubtedly they feel that the League of Nations needs us. (*Another laugh.*) It's important that we get there at once. So, Captain, I'll be grateful for prompt action.

CAPTAIN (*looking at the first passport*)
Miss Shirley Laughlin.

HARRY
Laughlin. This is Shirley. Step up, honey. (SHIRLEY *steps forward.*)

CAPTAIN (*pleased with* SHIRLEY)
How do you do?

SHIRLEY
Pleased to meet you.

CAPTAIN
This photograph hardly does you justice.

SHIRLEY
I know. It's terrible, isn't it!

HARRY (*interrupting*)
Who's next, Captain?

CAPTAIN
Miss Beulah Tremoyne.

HARRY
Come on, Beulah. (*She comes forward in a wide sweep, as* SHIRLEY *goes up and joins the group.*) Beulah is our bubble dancer, a product of the æsthetic school, and therefore more of a dreamer.

CAPTAIN

Exquisite!

BEULAH

Thank you *ever* so much. (*She starts to sit down by the* CAPTAIN. *She is turning it on.*)

HARRY

That'll be all, Beulah.

CAPTAIN

Miss Elaine Messiger——

HARRY

Come on, babe.

CAPTAIN

Miss Francine Merle——

HARRY

No tricks, Francine. This is just identification.

CAPTAIN

Miss Edna Creesh——

HARRY

Turn it off, honey.

CAPTAIN

And Miss Bebe Gould.

HARRY

You'll find Bebe a very, very lovely girl.

BEBE (*remonstrating*)

Harry!

HARRY

A shimmy artiste, and incorrigibly unsophisticated.

CAPTAIN (*summing up*)

Very beautiful. Very, very beautiful. Mr. Van, I congratulate you.

HARRY

That's nice of you, Captain. Now, can we . . .

CAPTAIN

And I wish I, too, were going to Geneva. (*He hands back the passports to* HARRY.)

HARRY

Then it's O.K. for us to pass?

CAPTAIN

But won't you young ladies sit down?

SHIRLEY

Thanks, Captain.

BEULAH

We'd love to.

FRANCINE

He's cute.

EDNA

I'll say.
(*They all sit.*)

HARRY

I don't want to seem oblivious of your courtesy,

Captain, but the fact is we can't afford to hang around here any longer. That train may pull out and leave us.

CAPTAIN

I give you my word, that train will not move to-night, and maybe not to-morrow night, and maybe never. (*He bows deeply.*) It is a matter of the deepest personal regret to me, Mr. Van, but——

HARRY

Listen, pal. Could you stop being polite for just a moment, and tell us how do we get to Geneva?

CAPTAIN

That is not for me to say. I am as powerless as you are, Mr. Van. I, too, am a pawn. (*He picks up his coat and hat.*) But, speaking for myself, I shall not be sorry if you and your beautiful companions are forced to remain here indefinitely. (*He salutes the girls, smiles and goes out.*)

HARRY

Did you hear that? He says he's a pawn.

BEBE

He's a Wop.

BEULAH

But he's cute!

SHIRLEY

Personally, I'd just as soon stay here. I'm sick of the slats on those stinking day coaches.

HARRY

After the way we've been betrayed in the Balkans, we can't afford to stay any place. (*He turns to* DON.) What's the matter, anyway? Why can't decent respectable people be allowed to go about their legitimate business?

DON

Evidently you're not fully aware of the international situation.

HARRY

I'm fully aware that the international situation is always regrettable. But what's wrong now?

DON

Haven't you been reading the papers?

HARRY

In Bulgaria and Jugo-Slavia? (*He looks around at the girls, who laugh.*) No.

DON

It may be difficult for you to understand, Mr. Van, but we happen to be on the brink of a frightful calamity.

HARRY

What?

DON

We're on the verge of War.

SHIRLEY

War?

BEBE

What about?

HARRY

You mean—that business in Africa?

DON

Far more serious than that! *World* war! All of them!

HARRY

No lie! You mean—it'll be started by people like that? (*Points after the* CAPTAIN.) Italians?

DON

Yes. They've reached the breaking point.

HARRY

I don't believe it. I don't believe that people like that would take on the job of licking the world. They're too romantic.

(PITTALUGA *steps forward.*)

PITTALUGA

Do you wish rooms, Signor?

HARRY

What have you got?

PITTALUGA

We can give you grande luxe accommodations, rooms with baths. . . .

HARRY

What's your scale of prices?

PITTALUGA

From fifty lira up.

DON

That's about five dollars a day.

HARRY (*wincing*)

What?

DON

Meals included.

HARRY

I take it there's the usual professional discount.

PITTALUGA (*to* DON)

Che cosa significa?

DON

Mr. Van and the young ladies are artists.

PITTALUGA

Ebbene?

DON (*scornfully*)

In America we give special rates to artists.

PITTALUGA (*grimly*)

Non posso, non posso.

(*The* CHERRYS *appear on the balcony above.*)

DON

I'm sure Mr. Pittaluga will take care of you
nicely, Mr. Van. He will show you attractive rooms
on the *other* side of the hotel. They're delightful.

HARRY

No doubt. But I want to see the accommodations.

PITTALUGA

Step this way, please.

HARRY

Come on, girls. Now—I want two girls to a room, and a single room for me adjoining. I promised their mothers I'd always be within earshot. Put on your shoes, Beulah. (*He goes out right, followed by the* GIRLS, *and* DON.)

BEULAH (*as they go*)

Why's he kicking? I think this place is *attractive!*

SHIRLEY

Oh—you know Harry. He's always got to have something to worry about. (*They have gone.*)

MRS. CHERRY (*coming down*)

What an extraordinary gathering!

CHERRY

There's something I've never been able to understand—the tendency of Americans to travel en masse. (*They pause to admire the view and each other. He takes her in his arms and kisses her.*) Darling!

MRS. CHERRY

What?

CHERRY

Nothing. I just said, "Darling"! (*He kisses her again.*) My sweet. I love you.

MRS. CHERRY

That's right. (*She kisses him.*)

CHERRY

I think we're going to like it here, aren't we, darling?

MRS. CHERRY

Yes. You'll find a lot to paint.

CHERRY

No doubt. But I'm not going to waste any time painting.

MRS. CHERRY

Why not, Jimmy? You've got to work and——

CHERRY

Don't ask "why not" in that laboriously girlish tone! You know damned well why not!

MRS. CHERRY (*laughing*)

Now really, darling. We don't have to be maudlin. We're old enough to be sensible about it, aren't we!

CHERRY

God forbid that we should spoil everything by being sensible! This is an occasion for pure and beautiful foolishness. So don't irritate me by any further mention of work.

Mrs. Cherry

Very well, darling. If you're going to be stinking about it . . . (*He kisses her again.*)

(*The* Doctor *comes in from the right and regards their love-making with scant enthusiasm. They look up and see him. They aren't embarrassed.*)

Cherry

How do you do?

Doctor

Don't let me interrupt you. (*He rings a bell and sits down.*)

Cherry

It's quite all right. We were just starting out for a walk.

Mrs. Cherry

The air is so marvellous up here, isn't it?

Doctor (*doubtfully*)

Yes.

(Dumptsy *comes in from the right.*)

Cherry

Yes—we think so. Come on, darling. (*They go out at the back.*)

Doctor

Mineral water.

Dumptsy

Yes, sir.

(Quillery *comes in and sits at the left. He is*

small, dark, brooding and French—an extreme-radical-socialist, but still, French.)

DOCTOR

Not iced—warm.

DUMPTSY

If you please, sir. (*He goes out, left.*)
(*A group of five Italian flying corps officers come in, talking gaily in Italian. They cross to the bar entrance and go out.*)

FIRST OFFICER

Sono Americane.

SECOND OFFICER

Sono belle, proprio da far strabiliare.

THIRD OFFICER

Forse sarrano stelle cinematografiche di Hollyvood.

SECOND OFFICER

E forse ora non ci rincrescerà che abbiano cancellato la nostra licenza. (*They go into the bar.*)

HARRY (*coming in*)

Good afternoon.

DOCTOR

Good afternoon.

HARRY

Have a drink?

DOCTOR

I am about to have one.

HARRY

Mind if I join you? (*He sits down near the* DOCTOR.)

DOCTOR

This is a public room.

HARRY (*whistles a snatch of a tune*)

It's a funny kind of situation, isn't it?

DOCTOR

To what situation do you refer?

HARRY

All this stopping of trains . . . (DUMPTSY *enters from the bar and serves the* DOCTOR *with a glass of mineral water*) and orders from Rome and we are on the threshold of calamity.

DOCTOR

To me it is not funny. (*He rises with his mineral water.*)

HARRY

Get me a Scotch.

DUMPTSY

With soda, sir?

HARRY

Yes.

DUMPTSY

If you please, sir.

QUILLERY

I will have a beer.

DUMPTSY

We have native or imported, sir.

QUILLERY

Native will do.

DUMPTSY

If you please, sir. (*He goes out.*)

DOCTOR

I repeat—to me it is *not* funny! (*He bows.*)
You will excuse me.

HARRY

Certainly. . . . See you later, pal. (*The* DOC-
TOR *goes.* HARRY *turns to* QUILLERY.) Friendly
old bastard!

QUILLERY

Quite! But you were right. The situation *is*
funny. There is always something essentially
laughable in the thought of a lunatic asylum. Although, it may perhaps seem less funny when you
are inside.

HARRY

I guess so. I guess it isn't easy for Germans to
see the comical side of things these days. Do you
mind if I join you? (*He rises and crosses to the
left.*)

QUILLERY

I beg of you to do so, my comrade.

HARRY

I don't like to thrust myself forward—(*He sits*

down)—but, you see, I travel with a group of blondes, and it's always a relief to find somebody to talk to. Have you seen the girls?

QUILLERY

Oh, yes.

HARRY

Alluring, aren't they?

QUILLERY

Very alluring.

(DUMPTSY *comes in with the drinks and goes.*)

(HARRY *takes out his chewing gum, wraps it in paper, places it in a silver snuff box, which he shows to* QUILLERY.)

HARRY

That's a genuine antique snuff box of the period of Louis Quinze.

QUILLERY

Very interesting.

HARRY

It's a museum piece. (*Puts the box in his pocket.*) You've got to hoard your gum here in Europe.

QUILLERY

You've travelled far?

HARRY

Yeah—I've been a long way with that gorgeous array of beautiful girls. I took 'em from New York to Monte Carlo. To say we were a sensation in

Monte Carlo would be to state a simple incontro-
vertible fact. But then I made the mistake of ac-
cepting an offer from the manager of the Club
Arizona in Budapest. I found that conditions in
the South-East are not so good.

QUILLERY

I travelled on the train with you from Zagreb.

HARRY

Zagreb! A plague spot! What were you doing
there?

QUILLERY

I was attending the Labor Congress.

HARRY

Yeah—I heard about that. The night club people thought that the congress would bring in a lot
of business. They were wrong. But—excuse me—
(*Rises.*) My name is Harry Van.

QUILLERY (*rises*)

Quillery is my name.

HARRY

Glad to know you, Mr. ——?

QUILLERY

Quillery.

HARRY

Quillery. (*Sits.*) I'm an American. What's
your nationality?

QUILLERY

I have no nationality. (*Sits.*) I drink to your
good health.

HARRY

And to your lack of nationality, of which I approve.

(*They drink.* SIGNOR *and* SIGNORA ROSSI *come
in and cross to the bar.* ROSSI *is a consumptive.*)

ROSSI

Abbiamo trascorso una bella giornata, Nina.
Beviamo un po'?

SIGNORA ROSSI

Dopo tutto quell' esercizio ti farebbe male.
Meglio che tu ti riposi per un'oretta.

ROSSI

Ma, no mi sento proprio bene. Andiamo. Mi
riposerò più tardi. (*They go into the bar.*)

HARRY

I get an awful kick hearing Italian. It's beautiful. Do you speak it?

QUILLERY

Only a little. I was born in France. And I love
my home. Perhaps if I had raised pigs—like my
father, and all his fathers, back to the time when
Cæsar's Roman legions came—perhaps, if I had
done that, I should have been a Frenchman, as they

were. But I went to work in a factory—and ma-
chinery is international.

HARRY

And I suppose pigs are exclusively French?

QUILLERY

My father's pigs are! (HARRY *laughs.*) The
factory where I have worked made artificial limbs
—an industry that has been prosperous the last
twenty years. But sometimes—in the evening—
after my work—I would go out into the fields and
help my father. And then, for a little while, I would
become again a Frenchman.

HARRY (*takes out his cigarette case*)

That's a nice thought, pal. (*Offers* QUILLERY *a
cigarette.*) Have a smoke?

QUILLERY

No, thank you.

HARRY

I don't blame you. These Jugo-Slav cigarettes
are not made of the same high-grade quality of
manure to which I grew accustomed in Bulgaria.

QUILLERY

You know, my comrade—you seem to have a
long view of things.

HARRY

So long that it gets very tiresome.

QUILLERY

The long view is not easy to sustain in this short-sighted world.

HARRY

You're right about that, pal.

QUILLERY

Let me give you an instance: There we were—gathered in Zagreb, representatives of the workers of all Europe. All brothers, collaborating harmoniously for the United Front! And now—we are rushing to our homes to prevent our people from plunging into mass murder—mass suicide!

HARRY

You're going to try to stop the war?

QUILLERY

Yes.

HARRY

Do you think you'll succeed?

QUILLERY

Unquestionably! This is not 1914, remember! Since then, some new voices have been heard in this world—loud voices. I need mention only one of them—Lenin—Nikolai Lenin!

(*A ferocious looking* MAJOR *of the Italian flying corps comes in and goes quickly to the bar. As he opens the door, he calls "Attention!" He goes into the bar, the door swinging to behind him.*)

HARRY

Yes—but what are you going to do about people like *that?*

QUILLERY

Expose them! That's all we have to do. Expose them—for what they are—atavistic children! Occupying their undeveloped minds playing with outmoded toys.

HARRY

Have you *seen* any of those toys?

QUILLERY

Yes! France is full of them. But there is a force more potent than all the bombing planes and submarines and tanks. And that is the mature intelligence of the workers of the world! There is one antidote for war—Revolution! And the cause of Revolution gains steadily in strength. Even here in Italy, despite all the repressive power of Fascism, sanity has survived, and it becomes more and more articulate. . . .

HARRY

Well, pal—you've got a fine point there. And I hope you stick to it.

QUILLERY

I'm afraid you think it is all futile idealism!

HARRY

No—I don't. And what if I did? I am an idealist myself.

QUILLERY

You too believe in the revolution?

HARRY

Not necessarily in *the* revolution. I'm just in favor of any revolution. Anything that will make people wake up, and get themselves some convictions. Have you ever taken cocaine?

QUILLERY

Why—I imagine that I have—at the dentist's.

HARRY

No—I mean, for pleasure. You know—a vice.

QUILLERY

No! I've never indulged in that folly.

HARRY

I have—during a stage of my career when luck was bad and confusion prevailed.

QUILLERY

Ah, yes. You needed delusions of grandeur.

HARRY

That's just what they were.

QUILLERY

It must have been an interesting experience.

HARRY

It was illuminating. It taught me what is the precise trouble with the world to-day. We have be-

come a race of drug addicts—hopped up with false
beliefs—false fears—false enthusiasms. . . .

(*The four* OFFICERS *emerge from the bar, talking excitedly.*)

SECOND OFFICER

Ma, è state fatta la dichiarazone di guerra
attuale?

FIRST OFFICER

Caricheremo delle bombe esplosive?

THIRD OFFICER

Se la guerra è veramente in cominciata, allora
vuol dire che noi. . . .

FOURTH OFFICER

La guerra è in cominciata fra l'Italia e la
Francia.

(*All the above speeches are said together, as the*
MAJOR *enters from the bar.*)

MAJOR

Silenzio! Solo il vostro commandante conosce
gli ordini. Andiamo!

(*All five go out hurriedly.*)

QUILLERY (*jumps up*)

Mother of God! Did you hear what they were
saying?

HARRY (*rises*)

I heard, but I couldn't understand.

QUILLERY

It was about war. I know only a little Italian—
but I thought they were saying that war has already been declared. (*He grabs his hat.*) I *must*
go and demand that they let me cross the border!
At once! (*He starts to go.*)

HARRY

That's right, pal. There's no time to lose.

QUILLERY

Wait—I haven't paid. . . . (*He is fumbling for
money.*)

HARRY

No, no. This was my drink. You've got to
hurry!

QUILLERY

Thank you, my comrade. (*He goes out quickly.
Airplane motors are heard, off at the right.* HARRY
crosses to the window. DUMPTSY *comes in to remove the empty glasses.*)

DUMPTSY

Fine view, isn't it, sir?

HARRY

I've seen worse.

DUMPTSY

Nothing quite like it, sir. From here, we look
into four nations. Where you see that little village,

at the far end of the valley—that is Austria. Isn't that beautiful over there?

HARRY

Are you Italian?

DUMPTSY

Well, yes, sir. That is to say, I didn't used to be.

HARRY

What did you used to be?

DUMPTSY

Austrian. All this part was Austria, until after the big war, when they decided these mountains must go to Italy, and I went with them. In one day, I became a foreigner. So now, my children learn only Italian in school, and when I and my wife talk our own language they can't understand us. (*He gets* HARRY's *drink and brings it over to him.*) They changed the name of this mountain. Monte Gabriele—that's what it is now. They named it after an Italian who dropped poems on Vienna. Even my old father—he's dead—but all the writing on the gravestones was in German, so they rubbed it out and translated it. So now he's Italian, too. But they didn't get my sister. She married a Swiss. She lives over there, in Schleins.

HARRY

She's lucky.

DUMPTSY

Yes—those Swiss are smart.

HARRY

Yeah, they had sense enough to get over there in the first place.

DUMPTSY (*laughs*)

But it doesn't make much difference who your masters are. When you get used to them, they're all the same.

(*The Porter's bell rings.* PITTALUGA *appears.*)

PITTALUGA

Dumptsy! Dumptsy! Una gentildonna arriva. Prendi i suoi bagagli. Affretati!

DUMPTSY

Si, Signore. Vengo subito. (*He goes.*)

PITTALUGA (*claps his hands*)

Sciocco! Anna, Per Dio! Dove sei stata, va sopra a preparare la stanza.

(ANNA, *the maid, enters with towels.*)
Presto, presto!

(ANNA *runs up the steps, exits.* PITTALUGA *goes back into the lobby.*)

IRENE'S VOICE

Vieni, Achille.

DON (*coming in*)

This is our cocktail lounge, madame.

(IRENE *enters. She is somewhere between thirty and forty, beautiful, heavily and smartly furred in*

*the Russian manner. Her hair is blonde and quite
straight. She is a model of worldly wisdom, chic,
and carefully applied graciousness. Her name is
pronounced* "EAR-RAY-NA." . . . *She surveys the
room with polite appreciation, glancing briefly at*
HARRY.)

DON

Your suite is up there, madame. All this part of
the hotel is quite new.

IRENE

How very nice!

DON

We have our best view from this side of the hotel.
(*He goes to the window.* IRENE *follows slowly.*)
You can see four countries—Italy, Switzerland,
Austria and Bavaria.

IRENE

Magnificent!

DON

Yes—we're very proud of it.

IRENE

All those countries. And they all look so very
much alike, don't they!

DON

Yes—they do really—from this distance.

IRENE

All covered with the beautiful snow. I think the

whole world should be always covered with snow. It would be so much more clean, wouldn't it?

Don

By all means!

Irene

Like in my Russia. White Russia. (*Sighs, and goes up to the next landing.*) Oh, and—how exciting! A flying field. Look! They're bringing out the big bombers.

Don

Madame is interested in aviation?

Irene

No, no. Just ordinary flying bores me. But there is no experience in life quite so thrilling as a parachute jump, is there!

Don

I've never had that thrill, I'm ashamed to say.

Irene

Once I had to jump when I was flying over the jungle in Indo-China. It was indescribable. Drifting down, sinking into that great green sea of enchantment and hidden danger.

(Dumptsy *comes in.*)

Don

And you weren't afraid?

IRENE

No—no—I was not afraid. In moments like that, one is given the sense of eternity.

HARRY (*viciously*)

Dumptsy! Get me another Scotch.

DUMPTSY

Yes, sir.

HARRY

And put ice in it, this time. If you haven't got any ice, go out and scoop up some snow.

DUMPTSY

If you please, sir. (*He goes into the bar.*)

IRENE (*her gaze wandering about the room*)
But your place is really charming.

DON

You're very kind.

IRENE

I must tell every one in Paris about it. There's something about this design—it suggests a—an amusing kind of horror.

DON (*not knowing quite how to interpret that*)
Madame is a student of decoration?

IRENE

No, no. Only an amateur, my friend. An amateur, I'm afraid, in everything.

(*The siren sounds from off at the right.* IRENE, *near the top of the staircase, stops to listen.*)

IRENE

What is that?

DON

Oh—it's merely some kind of warning. They've been testing it.

IRENE

Warning? Warning against what?

DON

I believe it's for use in case of war.

IRENE

War? But there will be no war.

(PITTALUGA *enters from the lobby, escorting* ACHILLE WEBER—*which is pronounced* "VAY-BAIR." *He is a thin, keen executive, wearing a neat little mustache and excellent clothes. In his lapel is the rosette of the Legion of Honor. He carries a brief case.*)

PITTALUGA (*as they come in*)

Par ici, Monsieur Weber. Vous trouverez Madame ici . . .

IRENE (*leaning over the railing*)

Achille!

WEBER (*pausing and looking up*)

Yes, my dear?

Irene

Achille—there will be no war, will there?

Weber (*amused*)

No, no—Irene. There will be no war. They're all much too well prepared for it. (*He turns to* Pittaluga.) Where are our rooms?

Pittaluga

Votre suite est par ici, Monsieur. La plus belle de la maison! La vue est superbe!

Irene (*to* Don)

There, you see! They will not fight. They are all much too much afraid of each other.

(Weber *is going up the staircase, ignoring the view.* Pittaluga *is following.*)

Irene (*to* Weber)

Achille—I am mad about this place! Je rafolle de cette place!

Weber (*calmly*)

Yes, my dear.

Irene

We must be sure to tell the Maharajah of Rajpipla, Achille. Can't you imagine how dear little "Pip" would love this? (*They go out on the landing above.*)

Harry

Who was that?

Don (*impressed*)

That was Achille Weber. One of the biggest men in France. I used to see him a lot at St. Moritz.

(*There is a sound of airplane motors off at the right.*)

Harry

And the dame? Do you assume that is his wife?

Don (*curtly*)

Are you implying that she's not?

Harry

No, no—I'm not implying a thing. (*He wanders to the piano.*) I'm just kind of—kind of baffled.

Don

Evidently. (*He goes out.*)

(Harry *at the piano strikes a chord of the Russian song,* "Kak Stranna." Dumptsy *enters from the bar and serves* Harry *with Scotch. The offstage noise increases as more planes take the air.*)

Dumptsy (*at the window*)

Do you see them—those aeroplanes—flying up from the field down there?

Harry (*glances toward window, without interest*)

Yes—I see them.

Dumptsy

Those are the big ones. They're full of bombs,

to drop on people. Look! They're going north.
Maybe Berlin. Maybe Paris.

(HARRY *strikes a few chords.*)

HARRY

Did you ever jump with a parachute?

DUMPTSY

Why, no—sir. (*He looks questioningly at*
HARRY.)

HARRY

Well, I have—a couple of times. And it's nothing.
But—I didn't land in any jungle. I landed where
I was supposed to—in the Fair Grounds.

DUMPTSY (*seriously*)

That's interesting, sir.

(*The* ROSSIS *enter from the bar. He is holding
a handkerchief to his mouth. She is supporting
him as they cross.*)

SIGNORA ROSSI

Non t'ho detto che dovevi fare attenzione? Te
l'ho detto, te l'ho detto che sarebbe accaduto ciò.
Vedi, ora ti piglia un accesso di tosse.

ROSSI

'Scusatemi, Mina. (*Another coughing fit.*)

SIGNORA ROSSI

Va a sdraiarti. Dovresti riposarti a lungo. E
adopera il termometro. Scommetto che t'è aumen-
tata la temperatura. (*They go out.*)

DUMPTSY

That Signor Rossi—he has tuberculosis.

HARRY

Is he getting cured up here?
(*The* DOCTOR *appears on the landing above.*)

DUMPTSY

Ja. This used to be a sanatorium, in the old days. But the Fascisti—they don't like to admit that any one can be sick! (*He starts to go.*)

DOCTOR

Dumptsy!

DUMPTSY

Herr Doctor.

DOCTOR (*coming down*)

Mineral water.

DUMPTSY

Ja wohl, Herr Doctor.
(DUMPTSY *goes out, left. The* DOCTOR *sits down.* HARRY *takes one more look toward the gallery, where* IRENE *had been. He then looks at the* DOCTOR, *and decides not to suggest joining him. He starts to play* "Kak Stranna." *The* DOCTOR *turns and looks at him, with some surprise. The uproar of planes is now terrific, but it starts to dwindle as the planes depart.*)

DOCTOR

What is that you are playing?

HARRY

A Russian song, entitled "Kak Stranna," meaning "how strange!" One of those morose ballads about how once we met, for one immortal moment, like ships that pass in the night. Or maybe like a couple of trucks, side-swiping each other. And now we meet again! How strange!

DOCTOR

You are a musician?

HARRY

Certainly. I used to play the piano in picture theatres—when that was the only kind of sound they had—except the peanuts.

(DUMPTSY *brings in the mineral water and stops to listen, admiringly.*)

DOCTOR

Do you know Bach?

HARRY

With pleasure. (*He shifts into something or other by Bach.*)

DOCTOR (*after a moment*)

You have good appreciation, but not much skill.

HARRY

What do you mean, not much skill? Listen to this. (*He goes into a trick arrangement of* "The Waters of the Minnetonka.") "The Waters of the

Minnetonka"—Cadman. (*He goes on playing.*)
Suitable for Scenics—Niagara Falls by moonlight.
Or—if you play it this way—it goes fine with the
scene where the young Indian chief turns out to be
a Yale man, so it's O.K. for him to marry Lillian
("Dimples") Walker. (*Starts playing* "Boola,
Boola.")

DOCTOR

Will you have a drink?

HARRY

Oh! So you want me to stop playing?

DOCTOR

No, no! I like your music very much.

HARRY

Then, in that case, I'd be delighted to drink with
you. Another Scotch, Dumptsy.

DUMPTSY

If you please, sir. (*He goes out.*)

DOCTOR

I'm afraid I was rude to you.

HARRY

That's all right, pal. I've been rude to lots of
people, and never regretted it. (*He plays on,
shifting back into* "Kak Stranna.")

DOCTOR

The fact is, I am a man who is very gravely distressed.

HARRY

I can see that, Doctor. And I sympathize with you.

DOCTOR (*fiercely*)

You cannot sympathize with me, because you do not know!

HARRY

No—I guess I don't know—except in a general way.

DOCTOR

You are familiar with the writings of Thomas Mann. (*It is a challenge, rather than a question.*)

HARRY

I'm afraid not, pal.

(*The* DOCTOR *opens* "The Magic Mountain," *which he has been reading.*)

DOCTOR

"Backsliding"—he said—"spiritual backsliding to that dark and tortured age—that, believe me, is disease! A degradation of mankind—a degradation painful and offensive to conceive." True words, eh?

HARRY

Absolutely!

(DUMPTSY *comes in with the Scotch.* HARRY

gets up from the piano and crosses. DUMPTSY *goes.* HARRY *sits down with the* DOCTOR.)

DOCTOR

Have you had any experience with the disease of cancer?

HARRY

Certainly. I once sold a remedy for it.

DOCTOR (*exploding*)

There *is* no remedy for it, so far!

HARRY

Well—this was kind of a remedy for everything.

DOCTOR

I am within *that* of finding the cure for cancer! You probably have not heard of Fibiger, I suppose?

HARRY

I may have. I'm not sure.

DOCTOR

He was a Dane—experimented with rats. He did good work, but he died before it could be completed. I carry it on. I have been working with Oriental rats, in Bologna. But because of this war scare, I must go to neutral territory. You see, nothing must be allowed to interfere with my experiments. Nothing!

HARRY

No. They're important.

DOCTOR

The laboratory of the University of Zurich has been placed at my disposal—and in Switzerland, I can work, undisturbed. I have twenty-eight rats with me, all in various carefully tabulated stages of the disease. It is the disease of civilization— and I can cure it. And now they say I must not cross the border.

HARRY

You know, Doctor, it *is* funny.

DOCTOR

What's funny? To you, everything is funny!

HARRY

No—it's just that you and I are in the same fix. Both trying to get across that line. You with rats—me with girls. Of course—I appreciate the fact that civilization at large won't suffer much if *we* get stuck in the war zone. Whereas with you, there's a lot at stake . . .

DOCTOR

It is for me to win one of the greatest victories of all time. And the victory belongs to Germany.

HARRY

Sure it does!

DOCTOR

Unfortunately, just now the situation in Germany is not good for research. They are infected with the same virus as here. Chauvinistic nationalism! They expect all bacteriologists to work on germs to put in bombs to drop from airplanes. To fill people with death! When we've given our lives to *save* people. Oh—God in heaven—why don't they let me do what is good? Good for the whole world? Forgive me. I become excited.

HARRY

I know just how you feel, Doctor. Back in 1918, I was a shill with a carnival show, and I was doing fine. The boss thought very highly of me. He offered to give me a piece of the show, and I had a chance to get somewhere. And then what do you think happened? Along comes the United States Government and they drafted me! You're in the army now! They slapped me into a uniform and for three whole months before the Armistice, I was parading up and down guarding the Ashokan Reservoir. They were afraid your people might poison it. I've always figured that that little interruption ruined my career. But I've remained an optimist, Doctor.

DOCTOR

You can afford to.

HARRY

I've remained an optimist because I'm essentially

a student of human nature. You dissect corpses
and rats and similar unpleasant things. Well,—
it has been my job to dissect suckers! I've probed
into the souls of some of the God-damnedest speci-
mens. And what have I found? Now, don't sneer at
me, Doctor—but above everything else I've found
Faith. Faith in peace on earth and good will to
men—and faith that "Muma," "Muma" the three-
legged girl, really has got three legs. All my life,
Doctor, I've been selling phoney goods to people
of meagre intelligence and great faith. You'd
think that would make me contemptuous of the
human race, wouldn't you? But—on the contrary
—it has given *me* Faith. It has made me sure that
no matter how much the meek may be bulldozed
or gypped they *will* eventually inherit the earth.

(SHIRLEY *and* BEBE *come in from the lobby.*)

SHIRLEY

Harry!

HARRY

What is it, honey?

(SHIRLEY *goes to* HARRY *and hands him a
printed notice.*)

SHIRLEY (*excited*)

Did you see this?

HARRY

Doctor—let me introduce, Miss Shirley Laughlin and Miss Bebe Gould.

SHIRLEY

How do you do?

DOCTOR (*grunts*)

How do you do.

BEBE

Pleased to know you, Doctor.
(HARRY *looks at the notice.*)

SHIRLEY

They got one of those put up in every one of
of our rooms.

HARRY (*showing it to the* DOCTOR)

Look—"What to do in case of air-raids"—in
all languages.

DOCTOR

Ja—I saw that.

SHIRLEY

Give it back to me, Harry. I'm going to send
it to Mama.

HARRY (*handing it to her*)

Souvenir of Europe.

SHIRLEY

It'll scare the hell out of her.

BEBE

What's the matter with these people over here?
Are they all screwy?

HARRY

Bebe—you hit it right on the nose! (*Turns to the* DOCTOR.) I tell you, Doctor—these are very wonderful, profound girls. The mothers of tomorrow!

(*He beams on them.* BEULAH *comes in.*)

SHIRLEY

Oh—shut up!

BEULAH

Say—Harry . . .

HARRY

What is it, honey?

BEULAH

Is it all right if I go out with Mr. Navadel and try to learn how to do this ski-ing?

(WEBER *comes out on the gallery and starts down.*)

HARRY

What? And risk those pretty legs? Emphatically—no!

BEULAH

But it's healthy.

HARRY

Not for me, dear. Those gams of yours are my bread and butter. (WEBER *crosses. They look at him. He glances briefly at them.*) Sit down, girls, and amuse yourselves with your own thoughts.

(*The* GIRLS *sit.* WEBER, *at the left, lights his cigar. The* CAPTAIN *comes in, quickly, obviously worried.*)

CAPTAIN

I have been trying to get through to headquarters, Monsieur Weber.

WEBER

And when can we leave?

CAPTAIN

Not before to-morrow, I regret to say.
(IRENE *appears on the gallery.*)

WEBER

Signor Lanza in Venice assured me there would be no delay.

CAPTAIN

There would be none, if only I could get into communication with the proper authorities. But —the wires are crowded. The whole nation is in a state of uproar.

WEBER

It's absurd lack of organization.
(*The* PIANIST *and* DRUMMER *come in from the lobby. The* VIOLINIST *and* SAXOPHONIST *follow.*)

CAPTAIN (*with tense solemnity*)

There is good excuse for the excitement now, Monsieur Weber. The report has just come to us that a state of war exists between Italy and France.

HARRY

What?

CAPTAIN

There is a rumor of war between Italy and France!

HARRY

Rumors—rumors—everything's rumors! When are we going to *know?*

CAPTAIN

Soon enough, my friend.

DOCTOR

And what of Germany?

CAPTAIN

Germany has mobilized. (IRENE *pauses to listen.*) But I don't know if any decision has been reached. Nor do I know anything of the situation anywhere else. But—God help us—it will be serious enough for everyone on this earth.

(IRENE *joins* WEBER, *who has sat down at the left.*)

IRENE (*to* WEBER, *and straight at him*)

But I thought they were all too well prepared, Achille. Has there been some mistake somewhere?

WEBER (*confidentially*)

We can only attribute it to spontaneous combustion of the dictatorial ego.

IRENE (*grimly*)

I can imagine how thrilling it must be in Paris at this moment. Just like 1914. All the lovely soldiers—singing—marching—marching! We must go at once to Paris, Achille.

HARRY (*rises*)

What's the matter with the music, professor? Us young folks want to dance.

(ELAINE *and* FRANCINE *come in.*)

ELAINE

Can we have a drink now, Harry?

HARRY

Sure. Sit down.

(DON *enters, exuding gratification at the sight of this gay, chic throng. The* ORCHESTRA *starts to play* "Valencia.")

WEBER

Will you have a drink, Irene?

IRENE

No, thank you.

WEBER

Will you, Captain Locicero?

Captain

Thank you. Brandy and soda, Dumpsty.

Dumptsy

Si, Signor.

Bebe (*yells*)

Edna! We're going to have a drink!
(EDNA *comes in.*)

Weber

For me, Cinzano.

Dumptsy

Oui, Monsieur. (*He goes into the bar.*)

Doctor

It is all incredible.

Harry

Nevertheless, Doctor, I remain an optimist.
(*He looks at* IRENE.) Let doubt prevail through-
out this night—with dawn will come again the
light of truth! (*He turns to* SHIRLEY.) Come on,
honey—let's dance.

(*They dance.* DON *dances with* BEULAH. *The*
ORCHESTRA *continues with its spirited but frail*
performance of "Valencia." *There are probably*
"*border incidents*" *in Lorraine, the Riviera, Po-*
land, Czecho-Slovakia and Mongolia.)

Curtain

ACT II

ACT II

SCENE I

It is about 7:30 in the evening of the same day.
The CHERRYS *are seated, both of them dressed*
for dinner. AUGUSTE *is serving them cocktails.*

CHERRY

Thank you.

AUGUSTE

Thank you, Signor.

CHERRY

Has any more news come through?

AUGUSTE

No, Signor. They permit the wireless to say
nothing.

CHERRY

I suppose nothing really will happen.

AUGUSTE

Let us pray that is so, Signor. (AUGUSTE *goes*
into the bar. CHERRY *leans over and kisses his*
wife.)

CHERRY

My sweet . . . you're really very lovely.

MRS. CHERRY

Yes. (*He kisses her again, then lifts his glass.*)

CHERRY

Here's to us, darling.

MRS. CHERRY

And to hell with all the rest.

CHERRY

And to hell with all the rest. (*They drink, solemnly.*)

MRS. CHERRY

Jimmy——

CHERRY

What is it, darling?

MRS. CHERRY

Were you just saying that—or do you believe it?

CHERRY

That you're lovely? I can give you the most solemn assurance. . . .

MRS. CHERRY

No—that nothing is going to happen.

CHERRY

Oh.

MRS. CHERRY

Do you believe that?

CHERRY

I know this much: they can't start any real war without England. And no matter how stupid and blundering our government may be, our people simply won't stand for it.

MRS. CHERRY

But people can be such complete fools.

CHERRY

I know it, darling. Why can't they all be like us?

MRS. CHERRY

You mean—nice.

CHERRY

Yes—nice—and intelligent—and happy.

MRS. CHERRY

We're very conceited, aren't we?

CHERRY

Of course. And for good and sufficient reason.

MRS. CHERRY

I'm glad we're so superior, darling. It's comforting.

(HARRY *comes in from bar.*)

CHERRY

Oh—good evening, Mr. Van.

HARRY

Good evening. Pardon me— (*He starts to go.*)

CHERRY

Oh—don't run away, Mr. Van. Let's have some music.

Mrs. Cherry

Won't you have a drink with us?

Harry

No, thanks, Mrs. Cherry—if you don't mind. (*Sits down at the piano.*) I'm afraid I put down too many Scotches this afternoon. As a result of which, I've just had to treat myself to a bicarbonate of soda. (*Starts playing* "Some of these days.")

Mrs. Cherry

I love that.

Harry

Thanks, pal—always grateful for applause from the discriminating. (*Finishes the chorus and stops.*)

Cherry

Do play some more.

Harry

No. The mood isn't right.

Mrs. Cherry

I can't tell you what a relief it is to have you here in this hotel.

Harry

It's kind of you to say that, Mrs. Cherry. But I don't deserve your handsome tribute. Frequently, I can be an asset to any gathering—contributing humorous anecdotes and bits of homely philosophy. But here and now, I'm far from my best.

CHERRY

You're the only one here who seems to have retained any degree of sanity.

MRS. CHERRY

You and your young ladies.

HARRY

The girls are lucky. They don't know anything. And the trouble with me is that I just don't give a damn.

MRS. CHERRY

We've been trying hard not to know anything —or not to give a damn. But it isn't easy.

HARRY

You haven't been married very long, have you? I hope you don't mind my asking. . . .

CHERRY

We were married the day before yesterday.

HARRY

Let me offer my congratulations.

CHERRY

Thank you very much.

HARRY

It's my purely intuitive hunch that you two ought to get along fine.

CHERRY

That's our intention, Mr. Van.

MRS. CHERRY

And we'll do it, what's more. You see—we have one supreme thing in common:

HARRY

Yeah?

MRS. CHERRY

We're both independent.

CHERRY

We're like you Americans, in that respect.

HARRY

You flatter us.

MRS. CHERRY

Jimmy's a painter.

HARRY

You don't say!

MRS. CHERRY

He has been out in Australia, doing colossal murals for some government building. He won't show me the photographs of them, but I'm sure they're simply awful. (*She laughs fondly.*)

CHERRY

They're allegorical. (*He laughs, too.*)

HARRY

I'll bet they're good, at that. What do you do,
Mrs. Cherry?

MRS. CHERRY

Oh, I work in the gift department at Fort-
num's——

HARRY

Behind a counter, eh!

MRS. CHERRY

Yes—wearing a smock, and disgracing my
family.

HARRY

Well, what d'ye know!

MRS. CHERRY

Both our families hoped we'd be married in some
nice little church, and settle down in a nice little
cottage, in a nice little state of decay. But when
I heard Jimmy was on the way home I just dropped
everything and rushed down here to meet him—
and we were married, in Florence.

CHERRY

We hadn't seen each other for nearly a year—
so, you can imagine, it was all rather exciting.

HARRY

I can imagine.

MRS. CHERRY

Florence is the most perfect place in the world
to be married in.

Harry

I guess that's true of any place.

Cherry

We both happen to love Italy. And—I suppose—we're both rather on the romantic side.

Harry

You stay on that side, no matter what happens.

Mrs. Cherry (*quickly*)

What do you think is going to happen?

Harry

Me? I haven't the slightest idea.

Cherry

We've looked forward so much to being here with no one bothering us, and plenty of winter sports. We're both keen on ski-ing. And now— we may have to go dashing back to England at any moment.

Mrs. Cherry

It's rotten luck, isn't it?

Harry

Yes, Mrs. Cherry. That's what it is—it's rotten. (Quillery *enters from the bar, reading a newspaper.*) So they wouldn't let you cross?

Quillery

No!

HARRY

Is there any news?

QUILLERY (*glaring*)

News! Not in this patriotic journal! "Uncon-firmed rumors"—from Vienna, London, Berlin, Moscow, Tokyo. And a lot of confirmed lies from Fascist headquarters in Rome. (*He slaps the paper down and sits.*) If you want to know what is really happening, ask *him*—up there! (*Indicates the rooms above.*)

CHERRY

Who?

QUILLERY

Weber! The great Monsieur Achille Weber, of the Comité des Forges! He can give you all the war news. Because he *made* it. You don't know who he is, eh? Or what he has been doing here in Italy? I'll tell you. (*He rises and comes close to them.*) He has been organizing the arms indus-try. Munitions. To kill French babies. And Eng-lish babies. France and Italy are at war. Eng-land joins France. Germany joins Italy. And that will drag in the Soviet Union and the Japanese Empire and the United States. In every part of the world, the good desire of men for peace and decency is undermined by the dynamite of jingo-ism. And it needs only one spark, set off anywhere by one egomaniac, to send it all up in one final, fatal explosion. Then love becomes hatred, cour-

age becomes terror, hope becomes despair. (*The*
DOCTOR *appears on the gallery above.*) But—it
will all be very nice for Achille Weber. Because
he is a master of the one *real* League of Nations—
(*The* DOCTOR *slowly comes down steps.*) The
League of Schneider-Creusot, and Krupp, and
Skoda, and Vickers and Dupont. The League of
Death! And the workers of the world are expected
to pay him for it, with their sweat, and their life's
blood.

DOCTOR

Marxian nonsense!

QUILLERY

Ah! Who speaks?

DOCTOR

I speak.

QUILLERY

Yes! The eminent Dr. Hugo Waldersee. A
wearer of the sacred swastika. Down with the
Communists! Off with their heads! So that the
world may be safe for the Nazi murderers.

DOCTOR

So that Germany may be safe from its oppres-
sors! It is the same with all of you—Englishmen,
Frenchmen, Marxists—you manage to forget that
Germany, too, has a right to live! (*Rings hand-
bell on the table.*)

QUILLERY

If you love Germany so much, why aren't you
there, now—with your rats?

DOCTOR (*sitting*)

I am not concerned with politics. (AUGUSTE
enters from the bar.) I am a scientist. (*To* AU-
GUSTE.) Mineral water!

(AUGUSTE *bows and exits into the bar.*)

QUILLERY

That's it, Herr Doctor! A scientist—a servant
of humanity! And you know that if you were in
your dear Fatherland, the Nazis would make you
abandon your cure of cancer. It might benefit too
many people outside of Germany—even maybe
some Jews. They would force you to devote yourself to breeding malignant bacteria—millions of
little germs, each one trained to give the Nazi
salute and then go out and poison the enemy. You
—a fighter against disease and death—you would
come a Judas goat in a slaughter house.

(DON *has appeared during this.*)

CHERRY

I say, Quillery, old chap—do we have to have
so much blood and sweat just before dinner?

QUILLERY (*turning on him*)

Just before dinner! And now we hear the voice
of England! The great, well-fed, pious hypocrite!

The grabber—the exploiter—the immaculate butcher! It was *you* forced this war, because miserable little Italy dared to drag its black shirt across your trail of Empire. What do *you* care if civilization goes to pieces—as long as you have your dinner—and your dinner jacket!

CHERRY (*rising*)

I'm sorry, Quillery—but I think we'd better conclude this discussion out on the terrace.

MRS. CHERRY

Don't be a damned fool, Jimmy. You'll prove nothing by thrashing him.

QUILLERY

It's the Anglo-Saxon method of proving everything! Very well—I am at your disposal.

DON

No! I beg of you, Mr. Cherry. We mustn't have any of that sort of thing. (*He turns to* QUILLERY.) I must ask you to leave. If you're unable to conduct yourself as a gentleman, then . . .

QUILLERY

Don't say any more. Evidently I cannot conduct myself properly! I offer my apologies, Mr. Cherry.

CHERRY

That's quite all right, old man. Have a drink. (*He extends his hand. They shake.*)

QUILLERY

No, thank you. And my apologies to you, Herr Doctor.

DOCTOR

There is no need for apologizing. I am accustomed to all that.

QUILLERY

If I let my speech run away with me, it is because I have hatred for certain things. And you should hate them, too. They are the things that make us blind—and ignorant—and—and dirty. (*He turns and goes out quickly.* DON *goes with him.*)

MRS. CHERRY

He's so right about everything.

CHERRY

I know, poor chap. Will you have another cocktail, darling?

MRS. CHERRY

I don't think so. Will you, Doctor? (*He shakes his head, indicates the mineral water. She rises.*) Let's dine.

CHERRY

It will be a bit difficult to summon up much relish. (*They go out, hand in hand.*)

HARRY

I find them very appealing, don't you, Doctor? (*The* DOCTOR *doesn't announce his findings.*) Did you know they were married only the day before yesterday? Yeah—they got themselves sealed in Florence—because they love Italy. And they came here hoping to spend their honeymoon on skis. . . . Kind of pathetic, isn't it?

DOCTOR

What did you say?

HARRY

Nothing, pal. (DON *comes in.*) Only making conversation.

DOCTOR (*rising*)

That Communist! Making me a criminal because I am a German!

DON

I'm dreadfully sorry, Dr. Waldersee. We never should have allowed the ill-bred little cad to come in here.

DOCTOR

Oh— It's no matter. I have heard too many Hymns of Hate before this. To be a German is to be used to insults, and injuries. (*He goes out. DON starts to go out left.*)

HARRY

Just a minute, Don.

DON

Well?

HARRY

Have you found out yet who that dame is?

DON

What "dame"?

HARRY

That Russian number with Weber.

DON

I have not enquired as to her identity.

HARRY

But did he register her as his wife?

DON

They registered separately! And if it's not too much to ask, might I suggest that you mind your own damned business?

HARRY

You might suggest just that. And I should still be troubled by one of the most tantalizing of questions—namely, "Where have I seen that face before?" Generally, it turns out to be someone who was in the second row one night, yawning.

DON

I'm sure that such is the case now. (*He starts again to go.*)

HARRY

One moment, Don. There's something else.

DON (*impatiently*)

What is it?

HARRY

I take it that your job here is something like that of a professional greeter.

DON

You're at liberty to call it that, if you choose.

HARRY

You're a sort of Y.M.C.A. secretary—who sees to it that all the guests get together and have a good time.

DON

Well?

HARRY

Well—do you think you're doing a very good job of it right now?

DON (*simply furious*)

Have you any suggestions for improving the performance of my duties?

HARRY

Yes, Don—I have.

DON

And I'd very much like to know just exactly who the hell do you think you are to be offering criticism of my work?

HARRY

Please, please! You needn't scream at me. I'm

merely trying to be helpful. I'm making you an offer.

Don

What is it?

Harry (*looking around*)

I see you've got a color wheel here. (*Referring to the light.*)

Don

We use it during the supper dance. But—if you don't mind, I——

Harry

I see—well—how would it be if I and the girls put on part of our act here, to-night? For purposes of wholesome merriment and relieving the general tension?

Don

What kind of an act is it?

Harry

And don't say, "What kind of an act," in that tone of voice. It's good enough for this place. Those girls have played before the King of Rumania. And if some of my suspicions are correct —but I won't pursue that subject. All that need concern you is that we can adjust ourselves to our audience, and to-night we'll omit the bubble dance and the number in which little Bebe does a shimmy in a costume composed of detachable gardenias, unless there's a special request for it.

Don

Do you expect to be paid for this?

Harry

Certainly not. I'm making this offer out of the goodness of my heart. Of course, if you want to make any appropriate adjustment on our hotel bill . . .

Don

And you'll give me your guarantee that there'll be no vulgarity?

(Irene *appears on the gallery and starts to come down. She is wearing a dinner dress.*)

Harry

Now be careful, Don. One more word like that and the offer is withdrawn . . .

(Don *cautions him to silence.*)

Don

It's a splendid idea, Mr. Van. We'll all greatly appreciate your little entertainment, I'm sure. (*To* Irene.) Good evening, Madame.

Irene (*with the utmost graciousness*)

Good evening, Mr. Navadel. (*She pauses at the window.*) It *is* a lovely view. It's like a landscape on the moon.

Don

Yes—yes. That's exactly what it's like.

(*She comes down.*)

HARRY

You understand, we'll have to rehearse with the orchestra.

DON

Oh, yes—Mr. Van. Our staff will be glad to co-operate in every way. . . . Do sit down, Madame.

IRENE (*sitting*)

What became of those planes that flew off this afternoon? I haven't heard them come back. (*Takes out a cigarette.*)

DON

I imagine they were moving to some base farther from the frontier. I hope so. They always made the most appalling racket. (*Lights her cigarette for her.*)

HARRY

About eleven o'clock?

(WEBER *appears on the gallery.*)

DON

Yes, Mr. Van. Eleven will do nicely. You'll have a cocktail, Madame?

(HARRY *goes into the lobby.*)

IRENE

No, no. Vodka, if you please.

DON

I shall have it sent right in. (*He goes off at*

the left into bar. IRENE *looks slowly off, after*
HARRY. *She smiles slightly.* WEBER *comes down*
the stairs quickly. He is not in evening dress. He
too pauses at the window.)

WEBER

A perfectly cloudless night! They're very lucky.
(*He comes on down.*)

IRENE

Did you get your call?

WEBER

Yes. I talked to Lanza.

IRENE

I gather the news is, as usual, good.

WEBER

It is extremely serious! You saw those bombers
that left here this afternoon?

IRENE

Yes.

WEBER

They were headed for Paris. Italy is evidently
in a great hurry to deliver the first blow.

IRENE

How soon may we leave here?

WEBER

None too soon, I can assure you. The French

high command will know that the bombers come
from this field. There will be reprisals—probably
within the next twenty-four hours.

IRENE

That will be exciting to see.

WEBER

An air raid?

IRENE

Yes—with bombs bursting in the snow. Sending
up great geysers of diamonds.

WEBER

Or perhaps great geysers of us.

IRENE *(after a moment)*

I suppose many people in Paris are being killed
now.

WEBER

I'm afraid so. Unless the Italians bungle it.

IRENE

Perhaps your sister—Madame d'Hilaire—perhaps she and her darling little children are now
dying.

WEBER *(sharply)*

My sister and her family are in Montbeliard.

IRENE

But you said the Italians might bungle it. They
might drop their bombs on the wrong place.

WEBER

I appreciate your solicitude, my dear. But you can save your condolences until they are needed. (DUMPTSY *comes in from the bar and serves the vodka.* WEBER *rises.*) I must telegraph to Joseph to have the house ready. It will be rather cold in Biarritz now—but far healthier than Paris. You are going in to dinner now?

IRENE

Yes.

WEBER

I shall join you later. (*He goes out.* DUMPTSY *picks up the* CHERRYS' *glasses.*)

DUMPTSY

We will have a great treat to-night, Madame.

IRENE

Really?

DUMPTSY

That American impresario, that Mr. Harry Van—he will give us an entertainment with his dancing girls.

IRENE

Is he employed here regularly?

DUMPTSY

Oh, no, Madame. He is just passing, like you. This is a special treat. It will be very fine.

IRENE

Let us hope so. (*She downs the vodka.*)

DUMPTSY

Madame is Russian, if I may say so.

IRENE (*pleased*)

How did you know that I am Russian? Just because I am having vodka?

DUMPTSY

No, Madame. Many people try to drink vodka. But only true Russians can do it gracefully. You see—I was a prisoner with your people in the war. I liked them.

IRENE

You're very charming. What is your name?

DUMPTSY

I am called Dumptsy, Madame.

IRENE

Are you going again to the war, Dumptsy?

DUMPTSY

If they tell me to, Madame.

IRENE

You will enjoy being a soldier?

DUMPTSY

Yes—if I'm taken prisoner soon enough.

IRENE

And who do you think will win?

Dumptsy

I can't think, Madame. It is all very doubtful. But one thing I can tell you: whoever wins, it will be the same as last time—Austria will lose.

Irene

They will all lose, Dumptsy. (*The* Cherrys *come in. She greets them pleasantly.*) Good evening.

Cherry

Good evening, Madame.

(*The* Cherrys *start to sit, across from* Irene.)

Irene

Bring some more vodka, Dumptsy. Perhaps Mr. and Mrs. Cherry will have some, too.

Cherry

Why, thank you—we . . .

Mrs. Cherry

I'd love to. I've never tasted vodka.

Irene

Ah—then it's high time. Bring in the bottle, Dumptsy.

Dumptsy

Yes, Madame. (*He goes in to the bar.*)

Irene

Come, sit down here. (*The* Cherrys *sits by her.*) You will find vodka a perfect stimulant to the appetite. So much better than that hybrid atrocity, the American cocktail!

CHERRY

To tell you the truth, Madame—we've already dined.

IRENE

It is no matter. It is just as good as a liqueur.

MRS. CHERRY

We didn't really dine at all. We merely looked at the minestrone and the Parmesan cheese—and we felt too depressed to eat anything.

IRENE

It's the altitude. After the first exhilaration there comes a depressive reaction, especially for you, who are accustomed to the heavy, Pigwiggian atmosphere of England.

CHERRY

Pigwiggian?

IRENE

Yes, Pigwig—Oliver Twist—you know, your Dickens?

(DUMPTSY *enters from bar with a bottle of vodka and two more glasses, which he places on the table. He returns to the bar.*)

CHERRY

You know England, Madame?

IRENE (*fondly*)

Of course I know England! My governess was a sweet old ogre from your north country—and when I was a little girl I used to visit often at Sandringham.

CHERRY (*impressed*)

Sandringham?

MRS. CHERRY

The palace?

IRENE

Yes. That was before your time. It was in the reign of dear, gay King Edward, and the beautiful Alexandra. (*She sighs a little for those days.*) I used to have such fun playing with my cousin David. He used to try to teach me to play cricket, and when I couldn't swing the bat properly, he said, "Oh, you Russians will never be civilized!" (*Laughs.*) When I went home to Petersburg I told my uncle, the Tsar, what David had said, and he was so amused! But now—you must drink your vodka. (*They rise, and lift their glasses.*) A toast! To his most gracious Majesty the King. (*They clink glasses.*) God bless him.

CHERRY

Thank you, Madame.

(*All three drink and* MRS. CHERRY *coughs violently.*)

IRENE (*to* MRS. CHERRY)

No—no! Drink it right down. Like this. (*She*

swallows it in a gulp.) So! (*Refills the glasses from the bottle.*) The second glass will go more easily. (*They sit.*) I used to laugh so at your funny British Tommies in Archangel. They all hated vodka until one of them thought of mixing it with beer.

MRS. CHERRY

How loathsome!

IRENE

It was! But I shall be forever grateful to them —those Tommies. They saved my life when I escaped from the Soviets. For days and nights—I don't know how many—I was driving through the snow—snow—snow—snow—, in a little sleigh, with the body of my father beside me, and the wolves running along like an escort of dragoons. You know—you always think of wolves as howling constantly, don't you?

CHERRY

Why, yes—I suppose one does.

IRENE

Well, they don't. No, these wolves didn't howl! They were horribly, confidently silent. I think silence is much more terrifying, don't you?

CHERRY

You must have been dreadfully afraid.

IRENE

No, I was not afraid for myself. It was the thought of my father. . . .

MRS. CHERRY

Please! I know you don't want to talk about it any more.

IRENE

Oh, no—it is so far away now. But I shall never forget the moment when I came through the haze of delirium, and saw the faces of those Tommies. Those simple, friendly faces. And the snow—and the wolves—and the terrible cold—they were all gone—and I was looking at Kew Gardens on a Sunday afternoon, and the sea of golden daffodils —"fluttering and dancing in the breezes."

(WEBER *has come in with the daffodils.*)

WEBER

Shall we go in to dinner now, Irene?

IRENE

Yes, yes, Achille. In a minute. I am coming. (WEBER *goes.* IRENE *rises.*) Now—we must finish our vodka. (CHERRY *rises.*) And you must make another try to eat something.

CHERRY

Thank you so much, Madame. (*They drink.*)

IRENE

And later on, we must all be here for Mr. Van's entertainment—and we must all applaud vigorously.

MRS. CHERRY

We shall, Madame.

CHERRY

He's such a nice chap, isn't he?

IRENE (*going*)

Yes—and a real artist, too.

CHERRY

Oh—you've seen him?

IRENE

Why—yes—I've seen him, in some café chantant, somewhere. I forget just where it was. (*The three of them have gone out together. The light is dimmed to extinction. The curtain falls.*)

END OF SCENE ONE

SCENE II

About two hours later.

WEBER *is drinking brandy. The* CAPTAIN *is standing.*

CAPTAIN

I have been listening to the radio. Utter bedlam! Of course, every government has imposed the strictest censorship—but it is very frightening—like one of those films where ghostly hands suddenly reach in and switch off all the lights.

WEBER

Any suggestions of air raids?

CAPTAIN

None. But there is ominous quiet from Paris. Think of it—Paris—utterly silent! Only one station there is sending messages, and they are in code.

WEBER

Probably instructions to the frontier.

CAPTAIN

I heard a man in Prague saying something that sounded interesting, but him I could not understand. Then I turned to London, hopefully, and listened to a gentleman describing the disastrous effects of ivy upon that traditional institution, the oak.

WEBER

Well—we shall soon know. . . . There'll be no trouble about crossing the frontier to-morrow?

CAPTAIN

Oh, no. Except that I am still a little worried about madame's passport.

WEBER

We'll arrange about that. Have a cigar, Captain?

CAPTAIN

Thank you.

(IRENE *comes in as the* CAPTAIN *starts to light the cigar.*)

IRENE

Do you hear the sound of airplanes?

(*All stop to listen, intently. The sound becomes audible. The* CAPTAIN *shakes out the match, throws the unlit cigar on the table, and dashes to the window and looks upward.*)

CAPTAIN

It is our bombers. One—two—three. Seven of them. Seven out of eighteen. You will excuse me? (*He salutes and dashes out.*)

WEBER

Seven out of eighteen! Not bad, for Italians.

(IRENE *has gone to the window to look out.*)

IRENE

I'm so happy for you, Achille.

WEBER

What was that, my dear?

IRENE

I said—I'm so happy for you.

WEBER

But—just why am I an object of congratulation?

IRENE

All this great, wonderful death and destruction, everywhere. And you promoted it!

WEBER

Don't give me too much credit, Irene.

IRENE

But I *know* what you've done.

WEBER

Yes, my dear. You know a great deal. But don't forget to do honor to Him—up there—who put fear into man. I am but the humble instrument of His divine will.

IRENE (*looking upward, sympathetically*)

Yes—that's quite true. We don't do half enough justice to Him. Poor, lonely old soul. Sitting up in heaven, with nothing to do, but play solitaire.

Poor, dear God. Playing Idiot's Delight. The game that never means anything, and never ends.

WEBER

You have an engaging fancy, my dear.

IRENE

Yes.

WEBER

It's the quality in you that fascinates me most. Limitless imagination! It is what has made you such an admirable, brilliant liar. And so very helpful to me! Am I right?

IRENE

Of course you are right, Achille. Had I been bound by any stuffy respect for the truth, I should never have escaped from the Soviets.

WEBER

I'm sure of it.

IRENE

Did I ever tell you of my escape from the Soviets?

WEBER

You have told me about it at least eleven times. And each time it was different.

IRENE

Well, I made several escapes. I am always making escapes, Achille. When I am worrying about you, and your career. I have to run away from the terror of my own thoughts. So I amuse myself by studying the faces of the people I see. Just ordinary, casual, dull people. (*She is speaking in a tone that is sweetly sadistic.*) That young English couple, for instance. I was watching them during dinner, sitting there, close together, holding hands, and rubbing their knees together under the table. And I saw him in his nice, smart, British uniform, shooting a little pistol at a huge tank. And the tank rolls over him. And his fine strong body, that was so full of the capacity for ecstasy, is a mass of mashed flesh and bones—a smear of purple blood —like a stepped-on snail. But before the moment of death, he consoles himself by thinking, "Thank God *she* is safe! She is bearing the child I gave her, and he will live to see a better world." (*She walks behind* WEBER *and leans over his shoulder.*) But I know where she is. She is lying in a cellar that has been wrecked by an air raid, and her firm young breasts are all mixed up with the bowels of a dismembered policeman, and the embryo from her womb is splattered against the face of a dead bishop. That is the kind of thought with which I amuse myself, Achille. And it makes me so proud to think that I am so close to you—who make all this possible.

(WEBER *rises and walks about the room. At length he turns to her.*)

WEBER

Do you talk in this whimsical vein to many people?

Irene

No. I betray my thoughts to no one but you. You know that I am shut off from the world. I am a contented prisoner in your ivory tower.

Weber

I'm beginning to wonder about that.

Irene

What? You think I could interest myself in some one else——?

Weber

No—no, my dear. I am merely wondering whether the time has come for you to turn commonplace, like all the others?

Irene

The others?

Weber

All those who have shared my life. My former wife, for instance. She now boasts that she abandoned me because part of my income is derived from the sale of poison gas. Revolvers and rifles and bullets she didn't mind—because they are also used by sportsmen. Battleships too are permissible; they look so splendid in the news films. But she couldn't stomach poison gas. So now she is married to an anemic Duke, and the large fortune that she obtained from me enables the Duke to indulge his principal passion, which is the slaughtering of wild animals, like rabbits, and pigeons and rather small deer. My wife is presumably happy with him. I have always been glad you are not a fool as she was, Irene.

IRENE

No. I don't care even for battleships. And I shall not marry an anemic Duke.

WEBER

But—there was something unpleasantly reminiscent in that gaudy picture you painted. I gather that this silly young couple has touched a tender spot, eh?

IRENE

Perhaps, Achille. Perhaps I am softening.

WEBER

Then apply your intelligence, my dear. Ask yourself: why shouldn't they die? And who are the greater criminals—those who sell the instruments of death, or those who buy them, and use them? You know there is no logical reply to that. But all these little people—like your new friends—all of them consider me an arch-villain because I furnish them with what they want, which is the illusion of power. That is what they vote for in their frightened governments—what they cheer for on their national holidays—what they glorify in their anthems, and their monuments, and their waving flags! Yes—they shout bravely about something they call "national honor." And what does it amount to? Mistrust of the motives of

every one else! Dog in the manger defense of
what they've got, and greed for the other fellow's
possessions! Honor among thieves! I assure you,
Irene—for such little people the deadliest weapons
are the most merciful.

(*The* CHERRYS *enter. He is whistling* "Minnie
the Moocher.")

> ### IRENE
> Ah! Mr. and Mrs. Cherry!

> ### CHERRY
> Hello there. (*They come down.*)

> ### IRENE
> You have dined well!

> ### MRS. CHERRY
> Superbly!

> ### CHERRY
> We ate everything—up to and including the
> zabaglione.

> ### IRENE
> You can thank the vodka for that. Vodka never
> fails in an emergency.

> ### CHERRY
> And we can thank you, Madame, and do so.

> ### IRENE
> But—permit me to introduce Monsieur Weber.
> (WEBER *rises.*) Mrs. Cherry—Mr. Cherry.

(*They are exchanging greetings as* DON *comes in.*)

DON

We're going to have a little cabaret show for you now, Madame.

WEBER

I don't think I shall wait for it, my dear.

IRENE

But you must——

WEBER

I really should look over Lanza's estimates——

IRENE

Please, Achille—Mr. Van is an artist. You will be so amused.

WEBER (*resuming seat*)

Very well, Irene.

DON (*his tone blandly confidential*)

Between ourselves, I don't vouch for the quality of it. But it may be unintentionally amusing.

IRENE

I shall love it.

CHERRY

This is the most marvellous idea, Mr. Navadel.

DON

Oh, thank you. We try to contrive some novelty

each evening. If you'll be good enough to sit
here——

(DON *goes up to usher in the* ROSSIS *and direct
them to their seats. The musicians come in and
take their places. The* DOCTOR *comes in.* DUMPTSY
*is busily moving chairs about, clearing a space for
the act.* IRENE *and the* CHERRYS *chat pleasantly.*
ANNA, *the maid, appears on the gallery above to
watch the entertainment.*)

(HARRY *comes in. He is wearing a tight-fitting
dinner jacket, and carries a cane and a straw hat.*)

HARRY

All set, Don?

DON

Quite ready, whenever you are.

HARRY

Okey-doke. Give us a fanfare, professor. (*He
goes out. The band obliges with a fanfare.* HARRY
returns, all smiles.) Before we start, folks, I just
want to explain that we haven't had much chance
to rehearse with my good friend, Signor Palota,
and his talented little team here. (*He indicates the
orchestra with a handsome gesture.*) So we must
crave your indulgence and beg you to give us a
break if the rhythm isn't all strictly kosher. (*He
waits for his laugh.*) All we ask of you, kind
friends, is "The Christian pearl of Charity," to
quote our great American poet, John Greenleaf
Whittier. We thank you. Take it away! (*He

*bows. All applaud. He then sings a song—The
girls come on in costume and dance.*)

(*During the latter part of the act, the* CAPTAIN,
the MAJOR, *and four flying corps* OFFICERS *come
in. The latter are dirty and in a fever of heroically
restrained excitement. They survey the scene with
wonderment and then with delight, saying, in
Italian, "What's all this?" and "What brought
these blonde bambinos to Monte Gabriele?" etc.*
HARRY *interrupts the act and orders the orchestra
to play the Fascist anthem, "Giovinezza." The
officers acknowledge this graceful gesture with the
Fascist salute. The* GIRLS *wave back. The* CAPTAIN
gets the OFFICERS *seated and then goes to order
drinks.* HARRY *and the* GIRLS *resume.*)

(*At the end of the act, all applaud and the*
OFFICERS *shout "Brava—Bravissima" and stamp
their feet with enthusiasm. The* GIRLS *take several
bows and go.* HARRY *returns for a solo bow, waving his straw hat. One of the* OFFICERS *shouts, in
Italian, "We want the young ladies!"*)

CAPTAIN (*to* HARRY)

My friends wish to know respectfully if the
young ladies will care to join them in a little drink?

HARRY

Certainly! Come back in, girls. Get over there
and join the army! (*The* GIRLS *do so.*) Now, folks
—with your kind permission—I shall give the girls
an interlude of rest and refreshment and treat

you to a little piano specialty of my own. Your strict attention is not obligatory.

(*He starts his specialty, assisted by* Shirley *and* Edna. *The* Officers *don't pay much attention. Bottles of champagne are brought for them and the* Girls.)

(Weber *goes and speaks to the* Captain. *He beckons him up to the landing of the stairs where they converse in low tones, the* Captain *telling him about the air-raid.*)

(Harry's *act is interrupted by the entrance of* Quillery.)

QUILLERY (*to* Harry)

Do you know what has happened?

DON

I told you we didn't want you here.

PITTALUGA

We're having an entertainment here.

QUILLERY

Yes! An entertainment!

HARRY

If you'll just sit down, pal. . . . (*He and the* Girls *continue with their singing.*)

QUILLERY

An entertainment—while Paris is in ruins!

CHERRY (*rises*)

What?

DOCTOR

What are you saying?

QUILLERY

They have bombed Paris! The Fascisti have bombed Paris!

DON

What? But it can't be possible——

HARRY

Go on, Shirley. Keep on singing.

QUILLERY

I tell you—to-night their planes flew over and——

CHERRY

But how do you know this?

QUILLERY

It is on the wireless—everywhere. And I have just talked to one of their mechanics, who was on the flight, and saw, with his own eyes——

HARRY

Won't you please sit down, pal? We're trying to give you a little entertainment— (*Stops playing.*)

QUILLERY

For the love of God—listen to me! While you sit here eating and drinking, to-night, Italian planes dropped twenty thousand kilos of bombs on Paris. God knows how many they killed. God knows how much of life and beauty is forever destroyed! And you sit here, drinking, laughing, with *them*—the murderers. (*Points to the flyers, who ask each other, in Italian, what the hell is he talking about.*) They did it! It was their planes, from that field down there. Assassins!

(*The* OFFICERS *make a move toward* QUILLERY —*one of them arming himself with a champagne bottle.*)

HARRY (*comes down from the piano*)

We can't have any skull-cracking in this club. Hey, Captain, speak to your men before anything starts.

(*The* CAPTAIN *comes down to the* OFFICERS *and pacifies them.* CHERRY *comes down to stand by* QUILLERY.)

MRS. CHERRY

Jimmy! . . . You keep out of this!

QUILLERY

I say, God damn you! Assassins!

MAJOR AND FIRST AND THIRD OFFICERS
(*jump up*)

Assassini!

HARRY

Now listen, pal. . . .

SHIRLEY

Harry! Don't get yourself mixed up in this mess!

QUILLERY

You see, we stand together! France—England
—America! Allies!

HARRY

Shut up, France! It's O. K., Captain. We can
handle this——

QUILLERY

They don't dare fight against the power of England and France! The free democracies against
the Fascist tyranny!

HARRY

Now, for God's sake stop fluctuating!

QUILLERY

England and France are fighting for the hopes
of mankind!

HARRY

A minute ago, England was a butcher in a dress
suit. Now we're Allies!

QUILLERY

We stand together. We stand together forever.
(*Turns to* OFFICERS.) I say God damn you. God
damn the villains that sent you on this errand of
death.

CAPTAIN (*takes a few steps toward* QUILLERY)

If you don't close your mouth, Frenchman, we
shall be forced to arrest you.

QUILLERY

Go on, Fascisti! Commit national suicide. That's the last gesture left to you toy soldiers.

HARRY

It's all right, Captain. Mr. Quillery is for peace. He's going back to France to stop the war.

QUILLERY (*turns on* HARRY)

You're not authorized to speak for me. I am competent to say what I feel. And what I say is "Down with Fascism! Abbasso Fascismo!"

(*There is an uproar from the* OFFICERS.)

CAPTAIN (*ordinarily gentle, is now white hot with rage*)

Attenzione!

QUILLERY

Vive la France! Viv——

CAPTAIN

E agli arresti.

QUILLERY

Call out the firing squad! Shoot me dead! But do not think you can silence the truth that's in me.

CAPTAIN (*grabs* QUILLERY *from the left and calls the* FIRST OFFICER)

Molinari!

(FIRST OFFICER *grabs* QUILLERY *from the right. They start to take him out.*)

QUILLERY (*as he is being led out*)

The Empire of the Fascisti will join the Empire of the Cæsars in smoking ruins. Vive la France! Vive la France!

(WEBER *goes upstairs and exits. They have gone.*)

CHERRY (*to* HARRY)

You'd better carry on with your turn, old boy.

HARRY

No, pal. The act is cold. (*To the orchestra leader.*) Give us some music, Signor. (*The orchestra starts playing.*) Let dancing become general.

CHERRY

Let's dance, my sweet.

MRS. CHERRY

I can't bear to, Jimmy.

CHERRY

I think we should.

MRS. CHERRY

Very well, darling. (*They dance. The* OFFICERS *dance with the* GIRLS.)

HARRY (*goes over to* IRENE)

Would you care to dance?

IRENE

Why—why, thank you. (*She stands up, and*

they join the slowly moving mob. SHIRLEY *is singing as loud as she can. The color wheel turns so
that the dancers are bathed in blue, then amber,
then red.*)

CURTAIN

END OF SCENE TWO

SCENE III

Later that night.

IRENE *and* HARRY *are alone. She is sitting, telling the story of her life. He is listening with fascination and doubt.*

IRENE

My father was old. The hardships of that terrible journey had broken his body. But his spirit was strong—the spirit that is Russia. He lay there, in that little boat, and he looked up at me. Never can I forget his face, so thin, so white, so beautiful, in the starlight. And he said to me, "Irene—little daughter," and then—he died. For four days I was alone, with his body, sailing through the storms of the Black Sea. I had no food—no water—I was in agony from the bayonet wounds of the Bolsheviki. I knew I must die. But then—an American cruiser rescued me. May God bless those good men! (*She sighs.*) I've talked too much about myself. What about you, my friend?

HARRY

Oh—I'm not very interesting. I'm just what I seem to be.

IRENE

C'est impossible!

119

HARRY

C'est possible! The facts of my case are eloquent. I'm a potential genius—reduced to piloting six blondes through the Balkans.

IRENE

But there is something that you hide from the world—even, I suspect, from yourself. Where did you acquire your superior education?

HARRY

I worked my way through college selling encyclopædias.

IRENE

I knew you had culture! What college was it?

HARRY

Oh—just any college. But my sales talk was so good that I fell for it myself. I bought the God-damned encyclopædia. And I read it all, travelling around, in day coaches, and depot hotels, and Fox-time dressing rooms. It was worth the money.

IRENE

And how much of all this have you retained?

HARRY (*significantly*)

I? I—never forget anything.

IRENE

How unfortunate for you! Does your encyclopædia help you in your dealings with the girls?

HARRY

Yes, Mrs. Weber. . . . I got considerable bene-fit from studying the lives of the great courtesans, and getting to understand their technique. . . .

IRENE

Forgive me for interrupting you—but that is not my name.

HARRY

Oh—pardon me, I thought . . .

IRENE

I know what you thought. Monsieur Weber and I are associated in a sort of business way.

HARRY

I see.

IRENE

He does me the honor to consult me in matters of policy.

HARRY

That's quite an honor! Business is pretty good, isn't it!

IRENE

I gather that you are one of those noble souls who does not entirely approve of the munitions industry?

HARRY

Oh, no—I'm not noble. Your friend is just another salesman. And I make it a point never to criticize anybody else's racket.

IRENE

Monsieur Weber is a very distinguished man. He has rendered very distinguished services to all the governments of the world. He is decorated with the Legion of Honor, the Order of the White Eagle, the Order of St. James of the Sword, and the Military Order of Christ!

HARRY

The Military Order of Christ. I never heard of that one.

IRENE

It is from Portugal. He has many orders.

HARRY

Have you ever been in America?

IRENE

Oh, yes—I've seen it all—New York, Washington, Palm Beach . . .

HARRY

I said America. Have you ever been in the West?

IRENE

Certainly I have. I flew across your continent. There are many White Russians in California.

HARRY

Did you ever happen to make any parachute landings in any places like Kansas, or Iowa, or Nebraska?

IRENE (*laughing*)

I have seen enough of your countrymen to know that you are typical.

HARRY

Me? I'm not typical of anything.

IRENE

Oh, yes, you are. You are just like all of them— an ingenuous, sentimental idealist. You believe in the goodness of human nature, don't you?

HARRY

And what if I do? I've known millions of people, intimately—and I never found more than one out of a hundred that I didn't like, once you got to know them.

IRENE

That is very charming—but it *is* naïve.

HARRY

Maybe so. But experience prevents me from working up much enthusiasm over any one who considers the human race as just so many clay pigeons, even if he does belong to the Military Order of Christ.

IRENE

If you came from an older culture, you would realize that men like Monsieur Weber are necessary to civilization.

HARRY

You don't say.

IRENE

I mean, of course, the sort of civilization that we have got. (*She smiles upon him benevolently. It is as though she were explaining patiently but with secret enjoyment the facts of life to a backward nephew.*) Stupid people consider him an arch-villain because it is his duty to stir up a little trouble here and there to stimulate the sale of his products. Do you understand me, my friend?

HARRY

I shouldn't wonder.

IRENE

Monsieur Weber is a true man of the world. He is above petty nationalism; he can be a Frenchman in France—a German in Germany—a Greek —a Turk—whatever the occasion demands.

HARRY

Yes—that little Quillery was an Internationalist, too. He believed in brotherhood, but the moment he got a whiff of gunpowder he began to spout hate and revenge. And now those nice, polite Wops will probably have to shut him up with a firing squad.

IRENE (*takes out a cigarette from her case*)

It is a painful necessity.

HARRY

And it demonstrates the sort of little trouble that your friend stirs up. (*He takes out his lighter and lights her cigarette.*)

IRENE

Do you know that you can be extremely rude?

HARRY

I'm sorry if I've hurt your feelings about Mr. Weber, but he just happens to be a specimen of the one per cent that I *don't* like.

IRENE

I was not referring to that. Why do you stare at me so?

HARRY

Have I been staring?

IRENE

Steadily. Ever since we arrived here this afternoon. Why do you do it?

HARRY

I've been thinking I could notice a funny resemblance to some one I used to know.

IRENE

You should know better than to tell any woman that she resembles somebody else. We none of us like to think that our appearance is commonplace.

HARRY

The one you look like wasn't commonplace.

IRENE

Oh! She was some one near and dear to you?

HARRY

It was somebody that occupies a unique shrine in the temple of my memory.

IRENE

That *is* a glowing tribute. The Temple of your memory must be so crowded! But I am keeping you from your duties.

HARRY

What duties?

IRENE

Shouldn't you be worrying about your young ladies?

HARRY

They're all right; they've gone to bed.

IRENE

Yes—but there are several Italian officers about. Aren't you supposed to be the chaperone?

HARRY

I leave the girls to their own resources, of which they have plenty. (*He stares hard at her.*) Have you always been a blonde?

IRENE

Yes—as far as I can remember.

HARRY

You don't mind my asking?

IRENE

Not at all. And now, may I ask you something?

HARRY

Please do so.

IRENE

Why do you waste yourself in this degraded work? Touring about with those obvious little harlots?

HARRY

You mean you think I'm fitted for something that requires a little more mentality?

IRENE

Yes.

HARRY

How do you know so much about me?

(*It should be remembered that all through this scene* HARRY *is studying her, trying to fit together the pieces of the jigsaw puzzle of his memory.*)

IRENE

For one thing, I saw your performance to-night.

HARRY

You thought it was punk?

IRENE

I thought it was unworthy.

HARRY

It was unfortunately interrupted. You should have seen . . .

IRENE

I saw enough. You are a very bad dancer.

HARRY

The King of Rumania thought I was pretty good.

IRENE

He is entitled to his opinion—and I to mine.

HARRY

I'll admit that I've done better things in my time. Would it surprise you to know that I was once with a mind-reading act?

IRENE

Really?

HARRY

Yeah.

IRENE

Now you're staring at me again.

HARRY

Have you ever been in Omaha?

IRENE

Omaha? Where is that? Persia?

HARRY

No. Nebraska. That's one of our states. I

played there once with the greatest act of my career. I was a stooge for Zuleika, the Mind Reader. At least she called me her stooge. But I was the one who had to do all the brain work.

IRENE

And she read people's minds?

HARRY

I did it for her. I passed through the audience and fed her the cues. We were sensational, playing the finest picture houses in all the key cities. Zuleika sat up on the stage, blindfolded—and usually blind drunk.

IRENE

Oh, dear. And was *she* the one that I resemble?

HARRY

No! There was another act on the same bill. A troupe of Russians . . .

IRENE

Russians?

HARRY

Singers, mandolin players, and squat dancers. One of them was a red-headed girl. She was fascinated by our act, and she kept pestering me to teach her the code. She said she could do it better than Zuleika.

IRENE

Those poor Russians. There are so many of

them all over the world. And so many of them
completely counterfeit!

HARRY

This dame was counterfeit all right. In fact,
she was the God-damnedest liar I ever saw. She lied
just for the sheer artistry of it. She kept after
me so much that I told her finally to come up to
my hotel room one night, and we'd talk it over.

IRENE

I hope you didn't tell her the code.

HARRY

No. After the week in Omaha the bill split. The
Russians went to Sioux Falls and we went on the
Interstate Time. I played with Zuleika for another year and then the drink got her and she
couldn't retain. So the act busted up. I've always
hoped I'd catch up with that red-headed Russian
again sometime. She might have been good. She
had the voice for it, and a kind of overtone of
mystery.

IRENE

It's a characteristic Gypsy quality. And you
never saw her again?

HARRY

No.

IRENE

Perhaps it is just as well. She couldn't have

been so clever—being duped so easily into going to your room.

HARRY

She wasn't being duped! She knew what she was doing. If there was any duping going on, she was the one that did it.

IRENE

She *did* make an impression!

HARRY (*looking straight at her*)

I was crazy about her. She was womanhood at its most desirable—and most unreliable.

IRENE

And you such a connoisseur. But—it's getting late.

HARRY (*rises*)

Do you know any Russian music? (*He crosses to the piano.*)

IRENE (*rises*)

Oh, yes. When I was a little girl my father used to engage Chaliapin to come often to our house. He taught me many songs.

HARRY

Chaliapin, eh? Your father spared no expense. (*He sits at the piano.*)

IRENE

That was in *old* Russia. (*He plays a few bars of* "Kak Stranna.") Kak Stranna!

HARRY

Yeah! How strange! (*He starts to play* "Prostchai.") Do you know this one? (IRENE *sings some of it in Russian.*) How do you spell that name—Irene?

IRENE

I-R-E-N-E. (HARRY *pounds the piano and jumps up.*) What's the matter?

HARRY

That's it! Irene! (*He pronounces it* I-REEN.)

IRENE

But what——?

HARRY

I knew it! You're the one!

IRENE

What one?

HARRY

That red-headed liar! Irene! I knew I could never be mistaken. . . .

IRENE

Irene is a very usual name in Russia. (*She laughs heartily.*)

HARRY

I don't care how usual it is. Everything fits together perfectly now. The name—the face—the voice—Chaliapin for a teacher! Certainly it's you! And it's no good shaking your head and looking amazed! No matter how much you may lie, you can't deny the fact that you slept with me in the Governor Bryan Hotel in Omaha in the fall of 1925. (IRENE *laughs heartily again.*) All right—go ahead and laugh. That blonde hair had me fooled for a while—but now I know it's just as phoney as the bayonet wounds, and the parachute jumps into the jungle. . . .

IRENE (*still laughing*)

Oh—you amuse me.

HARRY

It's a pleasure to be entertaining. But you can't get away with it.

IRENE

You amuse me very much indeed. Here we are —on a mountain peak in Bedlam. To-night, the Italians are bombing Paris. At this moment, the French may be bombing Rome, and the English bombing Germany—and the Soviets bombing Tokyo, and all you worry about is whether I am a girl you once met casually in Omaha.

HARRY

Did I say it was casual?

IRENE (*laughing*)

Oh—it *is* amusing!

HARRY (*angrily*)

I know you're amused. I admit it's all very funny. I've admitted everything. I told you I was crazy about you. Now when are you going to give me a break and tell me——

IRENE

You! You are so troubled—so—so uncertain about everything.

HARRY

I'm not uncertain about it any more, Babe. I had you tagged from the start. There was something about you that was indelible . . . something I couldn't forget all these years.

(WEBER *appears on the gallery, wearing his Sulka dressing gown.*)

WEBER

Forgive me for intruding, my dear. But I suggest that it's time for you to go to bed.

IRENE

Yes, Achille. At once. (WEBER *treats* HARRY *to a rather disparaging glance and exits.* IRENE *starts upstairs.*) Poor Achille! He suffers with the most dreadful insomnia—it is something on his mind. (*She goes up a few more steps.*) He is like Macbeth. Good night, my friend—my funny friend.

HARRY

Good night.

IRENE

And thank you for making me laugh so much
—to-night.

HARRY

I could still teach you that code.

IRENE

Perhaps—we shall meet again in—what was the
name of the hotel?

HARRY

It was the Governor Bryan.

IRENE

Oh, yes! The Governor Bryan! (*Laughing
heartily, she exits.* HARRY *goes to the piano, sits
down and starts to play* "Kak Stranna." DUMPTSY
enters from the bar.)

DUMPTSY

That was wonderful—that singing and dancing.

HARRY (*still playing*)

Thanks, pal. Glad you enjoyed it.

DUMPTSY

Oh, yes, Mr. Van—that was good.

HARRY (*bangs a chord*)

Chaliapin—for God's *sake!*

DUMPTSY

I beg your pardon, sir?

HARRY (*rises*)

It's nothing. Good night, Dumptsy. (*He goes out into the lobby.*)

DUMPTSY

Good night, sir. (*He starts for the bar.*)

CURTAIN

ACT III

ACT III

The following afternoon.

HARRY *is at the piano, idly playing the* "Caprice Viennoise," *or something similar. His thoughts are elsewhere.*

SHIRLEY *is darning some stockings and humming the tune.* BEBE *is plucking her eyebrows.*

BEULAH, ELAINE, FRANCINE *and* EDNA *are seated at a table.* BEULAH *is telling* ELAINE'S *fortune with cards. The others are watching. All are intensely serious, and all chewing gum.*

SHIRLEY

What's that number, Harry?

HARRY

The "Caprice Viennoise"—Kreisler.

SHIRLEY

It's pretty.

HARRY

You think so? (*He shifts to something jazzier.*)

BEULAH

You are going to marry.

ELAINE

Again?

139

BEULAH

The cards indicate dis*tinctly* two marriages, and maybe a third.

ELAINE (*chewing furiously*)

For *God's* sake!

SHIRLEY (*to* HARRY)

We certainly need some new stockings.

HARRY

We'll renovate the wardrobe in Geneva.

BEULAH

Now—let's see what the fates tell us next.

BEBE

Say, Harry—when do we lam it out of here?

HARRY

Ask Beulah. Maybe she can get it out of the cards.

BEBE

I hate this place. It's spooky.

BEULAH (*to* HARRY)

What'd you say, honey?

ELAINE

Ah—don't pay any attention to him. What else do they say about me?

BEULAH

Well . . . you'll enter upon a period of very poor health.

ELAINE

When?

BEULAH

Along about your thirty-seventh year.

SHIRLEY

That means any day now. (*She winks broadly at* BEBE, *who laughs.*)

HARRY (*vehemently*)

Listen to me, you nymphs! We can't be wasting our time with card tricks. We've got to do a little rehearsing.

SHIRLEY

Why, Harry—what are you mad about now?

HARRY

Who said I was mad about anything?

SHIRLEY

Well—every time you get yourself into a peeve, you take it out on us. You start in hollering, "Listen, girls—we got to rehearse."

HARRY

I am not peeved. Merely a little disgusted. The act needs brushing up.

BEBE

Honestly, Harry—don't you think we know the routine by now?

HARRY

I'm not saying you don't know it. I'm just saying that your performance last night grieved me and shocked me. You had your eyes on those officers and not on your work. That kind of attitude went big in Rumania, but now we're going to a town where artistry counts. Some day, I'll take the whole bunch of you to watch the Russian ballet, just to give you an idea of what dancing is.

(CAPTAIN LOCICERO *comes in.*)

CAPTAIN

Your pardon, Mr. Van.

HARRY

Ah, Captain. Good afternoon. . . . Rest, girls.

CAPTAIN (*to the* GIRLS)

Good afternoon.

GIRLS

Good afternoon, Captain.

HARRY

You bring us news?

CAPTAIN

Good news, I hope. May I have your passports?

HARRY

Certainly. (*He gets them out of his coat and hands them to the* CAPTAIN.)

CAPTAIN

Thank you. I hope to have definite word for you very shortly. (*He salutes and starts to go.*)

HARRY

What about Mr. Quillery, Captain? What's happened to him?

CAPTAIN

Mr. Quillery was very injudicious. Very injudicious. I am glad that you are so much more intelligent. (*He goes out.*)

SHIRLEY

I don't think they could have done anything cruel to him. They're awfully sweet boys, those Wops.

HARRY

So I observed. . . . Now listen to me, girls. Geneva's a key spot, and we've got to be good. Your audiences there won't be a lot of hunkies, who don't care what you do as long as you don't wear practically any pants. These people are accustomed to the best. They're mains—big people, like prime ministers, and maharajahs and archbishops. If we click with them, we'll be set for London and Paris. We may even make enough money to get us home.

BEBE

Oh—don't speak of such a thing! Home!

EDNA

To get a real decent henna wash again!

HARRY

The trouble with all of you is, you're thinking too much about your own specialties. You're trying to steal the act, and wreck it. Remember what the late Knute Rockne said: "Somebody else can have the all-star, all-American aggregations. All *I* want is a team!" Now, you—Beulah. You've got plenty of chance to score individually in the bubble number. But when we're doing the chorus routine, you've got to submerge your genius in the mass.

BEULAH

What do I do wrong, honey?

HARRY

Your Maxie Ford is lacklustre. Here—I'll show you. . . . (HARRY *gets up to demonstrate the Maxie Ford.*)

SHIRLEY (*laughs*)

If you do it that way, Beulah, you'll go flat on your face. Here—*I'll* show you.

HARRY

Just a minute, Miss Laughlin. Who's the director of this act, you or me?

SHIRLEY (*amiably*)

You are, you old poop. But you just don't know the steps.

ELAINE

Don't let her get fresh, Harry.

BEBE

Slap her down!

SHIRLEY

Give us the music, Harry.

BEULAH

Please, Harry. Shirley just wants to be helpful.

HARRY

I feel I should resent this—but— (*He returns to the piano.*) Go ahead, Miss Laughlin. Carry on. (*He plays.* SHIRLEY *demonstrates.* BEULAH *tries it.*)

BEULAH

Have I got it right?

SHIRLEY

Sure! He's just shooting his face off!

(*During this, the following conversation goes on:*)

ELAINE

You know that Wop that was giving me a play last night?

FRANCINE

You mean the one with the bent nose?

BEBE

I thought he was terrible. But that boy I had
is a Count.

ELAINE

Well, look what he gave me.

EDNA

What is it?

BEBE

Let me see it.

ELAINE

I don't know what it is.

BEBE

Looks like money. What kind of money is that,
Harry?

HARRY

It's an old Roman coin.

SHIRLEY

How much is it worth?

HARRY

I haven't looked up the latest rate of exchange
on dinars. But I think, dear, you've been betrayed. Now, pay attention, girls. . . . As I
said, we've got to improve the act, and with that
in view, I'm going to retire from all the dance
routine.

BEBE

What?

BEULAH

Why, *Harry*—we couldn't. . . .

SHIRLEY

Oh! I hurt you, didn't I! (*She rushes to him, coos over him.*) Yes, I did, you poor baby. I hurt his feelings—and I'm sorry—I'm very, very sorry.

HARRY

All right, Shirley. We can dispense with the regrets. Save your lipstick. (*He thrusts her away.*)

SHIRLEY

But why . . .?

HARRY

I've decided that I'm a thinker, rather than a performer. From now on, I shall devote myself to the purely creative end of the act, and, of course, the negotiation of contracts.

BEULAH

But when did you make up your mind to this, honey?

HARRY

I've been considering it for a long time.

SHIRLEY

Say! What were you talking about to that Russian dame?

HARRY

We discussed world politics.

FRANCINE

Oh!

SHIRLEY

And how are politics these days?

BEBE

Did you get anywheres near to first base, Harry?

HARRY

I find it impossible to explain certain things to you girls. You're children of nature.

SHIRLEY

We're *what?*

BEULAH

He means we're natural.

HARRY

Never mind, sweetheart. You'll sing the number, Shirley.

SHIRLEY

Me?

BEBE

With that terrible voice?

HARRY

She handled it fine that time I had bronchitis in Belgrade. And with a little rehearsal, you'll have the whole League of Nations rooting for you. Now—let's have it. (*He plays,* SHIRLEY *sings,* BEBE *disapproves.*)

(DON *comes in, dressed for travelling.*)

Don

Captain Locicero has got the orders to let us through and the train is due to leave about four o'clock. What a relief to be out of this foul place!

Harry

You going too, Don?

Don

Yes. There's nothing for me here. In fact, I'm sick and tired of Europe as a whole. I was in town this morning when they shot Quillery.

Bebe

Who?

Shirley

It was that little guy that bawled out the Wops.

Beulah

They *shot* him? Why did they have to do that?

Don

Of course, he asked for it. But even so, it's pretty sickening to see one of your fellow human beings crumpled up in horrible, violent death. Well —there'll be plenty more like him, and right here, too. The French know all about this air base, and they'll be over any minute with their bombs. So—it's California here I come!

Harry

And run right into the Japs? Better stop off at Wichita.

Don

I'll see you all on the train. (*He goes up the stairs.*)

Harry

You girls go get yourselves ready.

(*The* Cherrys *appear on the gallery.* Don *speaks to them, then goes out. The* Cherrys *come down.*)

Elaine

O.K., Harry.

Edna (*going*)

I'm surprised at those Wops. They seemed like such sweet boys.

Bebe

Sure—when they talk they sound like opera. But they're awful excitable. (Bebe, Elaine, Edna *and* Francine *have gone out.*)

Beulah

But I can't understand—why did they have to shoot that poor boy?

Harry

It's hard to explain, Beulah. But it seems there's some kind of argument going on over here, and the only way they can settle it is by murdering a lot of people.

Bebe

You don't need to tell *me* what it's like. I was in the Club Grotto the night the Purple Gang shot it out with the G's. And was that terrible! Blood all over everything! (*She and* SHIRLEY *and* BEULAH *have gone out.*)

HARRY

You heard what they did to Quillery?

CHERRY

Yes. It seems that he died like a true patriot, shouting "Vive La France."

HARRY

Better if he died like a man—sticking to what he knew was right.

CHERRY

He was a nice little chap.

MRS. CHERRY

The Italians are swine!

(DON *reappears on the balcony and comes down.*)

CHERRY

Oh, they had a perfect right to do it.

MRS. CHERRY

But to kill a man for saying what he thinks!

CHERRY

Many people will be killed for less than that.

HARRY

I'll have to be saying good-bye pretty soon. Did you say the train goes at four, Don?

DON

Four o'clock. Correct! (*He goes.*)

HARRY

I hope all this unpleasantness won't spoil your winter sports.

CHERRY

Oh, that's all washed up. We're going, too—if they'll let us cross the border.

HARRY

So the honeymoon has ended already?

MRS. CHERRY

Yes—I suppose so.

CHERRY

England is coming into this business. We have to stand by France, of course. And so there's nothing for it but . . .

MRS. CHERRY

And so Jimmy will have to do his bit, manning the guns, for civilization. Perhaps he'll join in the bombardment of Florence, where we were married.

CHERRY

You know—after the ceremony we went into the Baptistery and prayed to the soul of Leonardo da Vinci that we might never fail in our devotion to that which is beautiful and true. I told you we were a bit on the romantic side. We forgot what

Leonardo said about war. Bestial frenzy, he called it. And bestial frenzy it is.

MRS. CHERRY

But we mustn't think about that now. We have to stand by France. We have to make the world a decent place for heroes to live in. Oh, Christ! (*She starts to sob.* CHERRY *rushes to her.*)

CHERRY

Now, now, darling. We've got to make a pretense of being sporting about it. Please, darling. Don't cry.

HARRY

Let her cry, the poor kid. Let her sob her heart out—for all the God-damned good it will do her. You know what I often think? (*He is trying to be tactful.*) I often think we ought to get together and elect somebody else God. Me, for instance. I'll bet I'd do a much better job.

MRS. CHERRY

You'd be fine, Mr. Van.

HARRY

I believe I would. There'd be a lot of people who would object to my methods. That Mr. Weber, for instance. I'd certainly begin my administration by beating the can off him.

CHERRY

Let's start the campaign now! Vote for good old Harry Van, and his Six Angels!

(*The* CAPTAIN *comes in with a brief-case full of papers and passports. He takes these out and puts them on a table.*)

CAPTAIN

Good afternoon, Mrs. Cherry. Gentlemen.

HARRY

Do we get across?

CAPTAIN

Here is your passport, Mr. Van—and the young ladies, with my compliments. They have been duly stamped. (*He hands them over.*)

HARRY

Thanks, Captain. And how about Mr. Weber and his—friend? Are they going, too?

CAPTAIN

I have their passports here. I advise you to make ready, Mr. Van. The train will leave in about forty-five minutes.

HARRY

O.K., Captain. See you later, Mr. and Mrs. Cherry. (*He goes.*)

CHERRY

O.K., Harry.

MRS. CHERRY

And what about us, Captain?

CAPTAIN

Due to a slight technicality, you will be permitted to cross the frontier. Here are your passports.

CHERRY

I can't tell you how grateful we are.
(WEBER *appears on the gallery.*)

CAPTAIN

You needn't be grateful to me, Mr. Cherry. The fact that you are allowed to pass is due to the superb centralization of authority in my country. The telegram authorizing your release was filed at 11:43 to-day, just seventeen minutes before a state of war was declared between Great Britain and Italy. I must obey the order of Rome, even though I know it's out of date. Is your luggage ready?

CHERRY

It's all out here in the hall. We're off now, Captain. Well, good-bye and good luck!

CAPTAIN

And good luck to you—both of you.

CHERRY

I need hardly say that I'm sorry about all this. It's really a damned rotten shame.

CAPTAIN

It is. All of that. Good-bye, my friend. (*He*

extends his hand and CHERRY *shakes it.*) Madame.... (*He extends his hand to* MRS. CHERRY.)

MRS. CHERRY

Don't call *me* your friend, because I say what Quillery said—damn you—damn your whole country of mad dogs for having started this horror.

CAPTAIN (*bows*)

It is not my fault, Mrs. Cherry.

CHERRY

It's utterly unfair to talk that way, darling. The Captain is doing his miserable duty as decently as he possibly can.

CAPTAIN (*tactfully*)

In this unhappy situation, we are all in danger of losing our heads.

MRS. CHERRY

I know . . . I know. Forgive me for the outburst. (*She extends her hand to the* CAPTAIN *and they shake.*) I should have remembered that it's everybody's fault.

CHERRY

That's right, my sweet. Come along. (*They go out.*)

CAPTAIN (*to* WEBER)

Frankly, my heart bleeds for them.

WEBER

They're young. They'll live through it, and be happy.

CAPTAIN

Will they? I was their age, and in their situation, twenty years ago, when I was sent to the Isonzo front. And people said just that to me: "Never mind, you are young—and youth will survive and come to triumph." And I believed it. That is why I couldn't say such deceiving words to them now.

WEBER

The cultivation of hope never does any immediate harm. Is everything in order?

CAPTAIN (*rises*)

Quite, Monsieur Weber. Here it is. (*He hands over* WEBER'S *passport.*)

WEBER

And Madame's?

(*The* CAPTAIN *picks up a document on foolscap.*)

CAPTAIN

This is an unusual kind of passport. It has given us some worry.

WEBER

The League of Nations issues documents like that to those whose nationality is uncertain.

CAPTAIN

I understand—but the attitude of Italy toward the League of Nations is not at the moment cordial.

WEBER

Then you refuse to honor Madame's passport?

CAPTAIN

My instructions are to accord you every consideration, Monsieur Weber. In view of the fact that Madame is travelling with you, I shall be glad to approve her visa.

WEBER

Madame is not travelling with me. She has her own passport.

CAPTAIN

But it is understood that you vouch for her, and that is enough to satisfy the authorities.

WEBER (*with cold authority*)

Vouch for her? It is not necessary for anyone to vouch for Madame! She is entirely capable of taking care of herself. If her passport is not entirely in order, it is no affair of mine.

CAPTAIN (*genuinely distressed*)

But—I must tell you, Monsieur Weber—this is something I do not like. This places me in a most embarrassing position. I shall be forced to detain her.

WEBER

You are a soldier, my dear Captain, and you should be used to embarrassing positions. Undoubtedly you were embarrassed this morning, when you had to shoot that confused pacifist, Quillery. But this is war, and unpleasant responsibilities descend upon you and on me as well. However . . . (*He sees* HARRY, *who is coming in.*) I shall attend to my luggage. Thank you, Captain. (*He goes out.*)

CAPTAIN

Don't mention it. (*To* HARRY.) The young ladies are ready?

HARRY

Yes—they're ready. And some of your aviators are out there trying to talk them into staying here permanently.

CAPTAIN (*smiling*)

And I add my entreaties to theirs.

HARRY

We won't have any more trouble, will we?

(*The* DOCTOR *appears on the gallery with coat, hat, books done in a bundle, and umbrella. He comes downstairs.*)

CAPTAIN

Oh, no, Mr. Van. Geneva is a lovely spot. All of Switzerland is beautiful, these days. I envy you going there, in such charming company.

HARRY

Hi, Doctor. Have you got the rats all packed?

DOCTOR

Good afternoon. I am privileged to go now? (*He puts down all of his belongings and crosses.*)

CAPTAIN

Yes, Dr. Waldersee. Here is your passport.

DOCTOR

Thank you. (*He examines the passport carefully.*)

HARRY

I can tell you, Doctor—I'm going to be proud to have known you. When I read in the papers that you've wiped out cancer and won the Nobel prize, and you're the greatest hero on earth, I'll be able to say, "He's a personal friend of mine. He once admired my music."

DOCTOR (*solemnly*)

Thank you very much. (*To the* CAPTAIN.) This visa is good for crossing the Austrian border?

CAPTAIN

Certainly. But you are going to Zurich?

DOCTOR (*rises*)

I have changed my plans. I am going back into Germany. Germany is at war. Perhaps I am needed. (*He crosses to pick up his coat.*)

HARRY

Needed for what?

DOCTOR

I shall offer my services for what they are worth.
(HARRY *goes to help him on with his coat.*)

HARRY

But what about the rats?

DOCTOR (*fiercely*)

Why should I save people who don't want to
be saved—so that they can go out and extermi-
nate each other? Obscene maniacs! (*Starts to
put on his gloves.*) Then I'll be a maniac, too.
Only I'll be more dangerous than most of them.
For I know all the tricks of death! And—as for
my rats, maybe they'll be useful. Britain will put
down the blockade again, and we shall be starv-
ing—and maybe I'll cut my rats into filets and
eat them. (*He laughs, not pleasantly, and picks
up his umbrella and books.*)

HARRY

Wait a minute, Doctor. You're doing this without thinking. . . .

DOCTOR

I'm thinking probably that remedy you sold is
better than mine. Hasten to apply it. We are
all diseased. . . .

HARRY

But you can't change around like this! Have

you forgotten all the things you told me? All that about backsliding?

Doctor

No, I have not forgotten the degradation of mankind—that is painful and offensive to conceive. (*He is going out.*) I am sorry to disappoint you about the Nobel prize. (*He has gone.*)

Harry

Good-bye, Doctor. (*He sits down, wearily.*) Why in the name of God can't somebody answer the question that everybody asks? Why? Why? Oh—I know the obvious answers, but they aren't good enough. Weber—and a million like him—they can't take the credit for *all* of this! Who is it that did this dirty trick on a lot of decent people? And why do you let them get away with it? That's the thing that I'd like to know!

Captain

We have avalanches up here, my friend. They are disastrous. They start with a little crack in the ice, so tiny that one cannot see it, until, suddenly, it bursts wide open. And then it is too late.

Harry

That's very effective, Captain. But it don't satisfy me, because this avalanche isn't made out of ice. It's made out of flesh and blood—and—and *brains*. . . . It's God-damned bad management—that's what it is! (*This last is half to himself.*)

(IRENE *has appeared on the gallery and started to come down.*)

IRENE

Still upset about the situation, Mr. Van? Ah —good afternoon, my dear Captain Locicero.

CAPTAIN

Good afternoon, Madame.

IRENE

I have had the most superb rest here. The atmosphere is so calm, and impersonal, and soothing. I can't bear to think that we're going to Biarritz, with the dull, dismal old sea pounding in my ears.

(WEBER *comes in.*)

IRENE

We are leaving now, Achille?

WEBER

I believe that some difficulties have arisen. (*He looks toward the* CAPTAIN.)

IRENE

Difficulties?

CAPTAIN

I regret, Madame, that there must be some further delay.

IRENE

Oh! Then the train is not going through, after all?

CAPTAIN

The train is going, Madame. But this passport of yours presents problems which, under the circumstances——

IRENE

Monsieur Weber will settle the problems, whatever they are. Won't you, Achille?

WEBER

There is some question about your nationality, Irene.

CAPTAIN (*referring to the passport*)

It states here, Madame, that your birthplace is uncertain, but assumed to be Armenia.

IRENE

That is a province of Russia!

CAPTAIN

You subsequently became a resident of England, then of the United States, and then of France.

IRENE (*angrily*)

Yes—it's all there—clearly stated. I have never before had the slightest difficulty about my passport. It was issued by the League of Nations.

Weber

I'm afraid the standing of the League of Nations is not very high in Italy at this moment.

Captain

The fact is, Madame, the very existence of the League is no longer recognized by our government. For that reason, we can not permit you to cross the frontier at this time. (*She looks at him and then at* Weber. *The* Captain *hands her the passport.*) I'm sure you will appreciate the delicacy of my position. Perhaps we shall be able to adjust the matter to-morrow. (*He salutes and goes out, glad to escape.* Harry *goes with him, asking "What's the trouble, Captain? Can't something be done about it?"*)

Weber

I should of course wait over, Irene. But you know how dangerous it is for me to delay my return to France by so much as one day. I have been in touch with our agents. The premier is demanding that production be doubled—trebled—at once.

Irene

Of course.

Weber

Here—(*He takes out an envelope containing money.*) This will cover all possible expenses. (*He gives her the envelope.*) There is a train for Venice this evening. You must go there and see Lanza. I have already sent him full instructions.

IRENE

Yes, Achille. And I thank you for having managed this very, very tactfully.

WEBER (*smiles*)

You are a genuinely superior person, my dear. It is a privilege to have known you.

IRENE

Thank you again, Achille. Good-bye.

WEBER

Good-bye, Irene. (*He kisses her hand.* HARRY *returns.*) Coming, Mr. Van?

HARRY

In a minute. (WEBER *goes.* IRENE *puts the money in her handbag.*) Tough luck, babe.

IRENE

It's no matter.

HARRY

I just talked to the Captain and he isn't going to be as brutal as the Bolsheviks were. I mean, you won't suffer any bayonet wounds. He'll fix it for you to get through to-morrow.

IRENE

You want to be encouraging, my dear friend. But it's no use. The Italian government has too many reasons for wishing to detain me. They'll see to it that I disappear—quietly—and completely.

HARRY

Yes—I know all about that.

IRENE

All about what?

HARRY

You're a person of tremendous significance.
You always were.

(SHIRLEY *appears at the left.*)

SHIRLEY

Hey, Harry! It's time for us to go.

HARRY

I'll be right out.
(SHIRLEY *goes.*)

IRENE

Go away—go away with your friends. If I am
to die, it is no concern of yours!

HARRY

Listen, babe—I haven't any wish to . . .

IRENE (*flaming*)

And please don't call me *babe!* (*She stands up
and walks away from him. He follows her.*)

HARRY

My apologies, Madame. I just call everybody
"babe."

IRENE

Perhaps that's why I do not like it!

HARRY

Even if I don't believe anything you say, I can see pretty plainly that you're in a tough spot. And considering what we were to each other in the old Governor Bryan Hotel——

IRENE

Must you always be in Omaha?

HARRY

I'd like to help you, Irene. Isn't there something I can do?

IRENE

I thank you, from my heart, I thank you, for that offer. But it's useless. . . .

HARRY

You don't have to thank me. Tell me—what can I do?

IRENE

You're very kind, and very gallant. But, unfortunately, you're no match for Achille Weber. He has decided that I shall remain here and his decision is final!

HARRY

Is he responsible for them stopping you?

IRENE

Of course he is. I knew it the moment I saw that ashamed look on Captain Locicero's face, when he refused to permit me . . .

HARRY

So Weber double-crossed you, did he! What has the son of a bitch got against you?

IRENE

He's afraid of me. I know too much about his methods of promoting his own business.

HARRY

Everybody knows about his methods. Little Quillery was talking about them last night. . . .

IRENE

Yes—and what happened to Quillery? That's what happens to every one who dares to criticize him. Last night I did the one thing he could never forgive. I told him the truth! At last I told him just what I think. And now—you see how quickly he strikes back!

(SHIRLEY *and* BEBE *appear.*)

SHIRLEY

Harry! The bus is going to leave.

HARRY

All right—all right!

BEBE

But we got to go this *minute!*

HARRY

I'll be with you. Get out!

SHIRLEY (*as they go*)

Can you imagine? He stops everything to make another pass at that Russian. (*They have gone.*)

IRENE

Go ahead—go ahead! You can't help me! No one can! (*He picks up his coat and hat.*) But—if it will make you any happier in your future travels with Les Blondes, I'll tell you, yes—I did know you, slightly, in Omaha!

HARRY (*peering at her*)

Are you lying again?

IRENE

It was Room 974. Does that convince you?

HARRY (*ferociously*)

How can I remember what room it was?

IRENE (*smiling*)

Well, then—you'll never be sure, Mr. Van.

BEBE'S VOICE

Harry!

SHIRLEY'S VOICE

For God's sake, Harry!

DON (*appearing*)

We can't wait another instant! (DON *goes.*)

SHIRLEY'S VOICE

Come *on!*

HARRY

(*He turns and starts for the door, addressing the* GIRLS *en route.*) All right, God damn it! (*He goes out.*)

(IRENE *takes out her vanity case, and does something to her face. She takes off her hat and cloak.* DUMPTSY *comes in from the back. He is wearing the uniform of a private in the Italian army,* with *gas mask at the alert, and a full pack on his back.*)

DUMPTSY

Good afternoon, Madame.

IRENE (*turning*)

Why, Dumptsy—what is that costume?

DUMPTSY

They called me up. Look! I'm an Italian soldier.

IRENE

You look splendid!

DUMPTSY

If you please, Madame. But why didn't you go on that bus?

IRENE

I've decided to stay and enjoy the winter sports.

DUMPTSY

I don't think this is a good place any more, Madame. They say the war is very big—bigger than last time.

IRENE

Yes—I hear that on all sides.

DUMPTSY

The French will be here to drop bombs on everybody.

IRENE

It will be thrilling for us if they do. Won't it, Dumptsy?

DUMPTSY

Maybe it will, Madame. But—I came to say good-bye to Auguste, the barman, and Anna, the maid. They're both cousins of mine. They'll laugh when they see me in these clothes. (*He goes to the left.*) Can I get you anything, Madame?

IRENE

Yes, Dumptsy. I'll have a bottle of champagne. Bring two glasses. We'll have a drink together.

DUMPTSY

If you please, Madame. (DUMPTSY *goes into the bar.* IRENE *lights a cigarette and goes up to the window to look out.* PITTALUGA *comes in.*)

PITTALUGA

Your luggage is in the hall, Madame. Will you wish it taken to the same suite?

IRENE

No—I didn't really care much for those rooms. Have you anything smaller?

PITTALUGA (*in a less deferential tone*)

We have smaller rooms on the other side of the hotel.

IRENE

I'll have the smallest. It will be cozier.

PITTALUGA

You wish to go to it now?

IRENE

No. You can send up the luggage. I'll look at it later.

(PITTALUGA *bows and goes.* DUMPTSY *returns with the champagne.*)

DUMPTSY

I was right, Madame. Auguste laughed very much.

IRENE (*coming down*)

What will happen to your wife and children, Dumptsy?

DUMPTSY

Oh—I suppose the Fascisti will feed them. They promised to feed all the families with a man who is out fighting for their country. (*He has filled her glass. She sits down.*)

IRENE

Go ahead and pour yourself one, Dumptsy.

DUMPTSY

Thank you so much, Madame. I wasn't sure I heard correctly.

IRENE

Here's to you, Dumptsy—and to Austria.

DUMPTSY

And to you, Madame, if you please.

IRENE

Thank you. (*They drink.*)

DUMPTSY

And may you soon be restored to your home in Petersburg.

IRENE

Petersburg?

DUMPTSY

Yes, Madame. Your home.

IRENE (*with a slight smile*)

Ah, yes. My home! (*They drink again.*) And have no fear for the future, Dumptsy. Whatever happens—have no fear!

DUMPTSY

If you please, Madame. (*He finishes his drink.*) And now I must go find Anna, if you will excuse me.

IRENE

Here, Dumptsy. (*She hands him a note of money.*) Good-bye, and God bless you.

DUMPTSY

Thank you so much, Madame. (DUMPTSY *leans over and kisses her hand.*) Kiss die hand, Madame.

(*The* CAPTAIN *and* MAJOR *come in from the lobby.* DUMPTSY *salutes, strenuously, and goes out. The* MAJOR *goes across and into the bar. The* CAPTAIN *is following him.*)

IRENE

Some champagne, Captain?

CAPTAIN

No, thank you very much.

IRENE

You needn't be anxious to avoid me, Captain. I know perfectly well that it wasn't your fault.

CAPTAIN

You are very understanding, Madame.

IRENE

Yes—that's true. I am one of the most remarkably understanding people on earth. (*She swallows her drink.*) I understand so damned much that I am here, alone, on this cold mountain, and I have no one to turn to, nowhere to go . . .

CAPTAIN

If I can be of service to you in any way . . .

IRENE

I know you'll be kind, Captain Locicero. And faultlessly polite.

CAPTAIN (*with genuine sympathy*)

I realize, Madame, that politeness means noth-

ing now. But—under these tragic circumstances
—what else can I do?

IRENE (*deliberately*)

What else can you do? I'll tell you what else you
can do in these tragic circumstances. You can refuse to fight! Have you ever thought of that possi-
bility? You can refuse to use those weapons that
they have sold you! But—you were going into the
bar. Please don't let me detain you.

CAPTAIN

You will forgive me, Madame?

IRENE

Fully, my dear Captain. . . . Fully.

CAPTAIN

Thank you. (*He salutes and goes into the bar.*)
(IRENE *pours herself another drink. Then she
picks it up, goes to the piano, and starts to play
a sketchy accompaniment for "Kak Stranna."
She seems to be pretty close to tears. Perhaps she
does cry a little, thoroughly enjoying the emotion.*
HARRY *comes in wearing his snappy overcoat and
his hat. He pays no attention to her, as he takes
off his coat and hat and throws them down somewhere.*)

IRENE

Did you have some trouble?

HARRY

No. Whose is that champagne?

IRENE

Mine. Won't you have some?

HARRY

Thanks.

IRENE

Dumptsy used that glass.

HARRY

That's all right. (*He fills the glass and drinks.*)

IRENE

What happened? Didn't the train go?

HARRY

Yes—the train went. . . . I got the girls on board. Mr. and Mrs. Cherry promised to look out for them. They'll be O.K.

IRENE

And you came back—to me?

HARRY (*curtly*)

It seems fairly obvious that I did come back. (*He refills his glass.*)

IRENE

You meant it when you said that you wanted to help me.

HARRY

You said I'd never be sure. Well—I came back

to tell you I *am* sure! I got thinking back, in the bus, and I came to the conclusion that it *was* Room 974 or close to it, anyway. And somehow or other, I couldn't help feeling rather flattered, and touched, to think that with all the sordid hotel rooms you've been in, you should have remembered that one. (*He has some more champagne.*)

IRENE (*after a moment*)

Bayard is not dead!

HARRY

Who?

IRENE

The Chevalier Bayard.

HARRY

Oh?

IRENE

Somewhere in that funny, music-hall soul of yours is the spirit of Leander, and Abelard, and Galahad. You give up everything—risk your life —walk unafraid into the valley of the shadow—to aid and comfort a damsel in distress. Isn't that the truth?

HARRY

Yes—it's the truth—plainly and simply put. (*He pours himself more champagne and drinks it quickly.*) Listen to me, babe—when are you going to break down and tell me who the hell are you?

IRENE

Does it matter so very much who I am?

HARRY

No.

IRENE

Give me some more champagne. (HARRY *goes to her and pours.*) My father was not one of the Romanoffs. But for many years, he was their guest—in Siberia. From him I learned that it is no use telling the truth to people whose whole life is a lie. But you—Harry—you are different. You are an honest man.

HARRY (*after a short pause*)

I am—am I? (*He crosses to the bar.*) Another bottle of champagne. . . . Hi, Captain.

CAPTAIN'S VOICE (*offstage in bar*)

What has happened, Mr. Van? Did you miss the train?

HARRY

No—just a God-damned fool. (*He closes the bar door.* IRENE *is gazing at him. He goes to her and kisses her.*)

IRENE

All these years—you've been surrounded by blondes—and you've loved only me!

HARRY

Now listen—we don't want to have any misunderstanding. If you're hooking up with me, it's only for professional reasons—see?

IRENE

Yes—I see.

HARRY

And what's more, I'm the manager. I'll fix it with the Captain for us to cross the border to-morrow, or the next day, or soon. We'll join up with the girls in Geneva—and that's as good a place as any to rehearse the code.

IRENE

The code! Of *course*—the code! I shall learn it easily.

HARRY

It's a very deep complicated scientific problem.

IRENE

You must tell it to me at once.

HARRY

At once! If you're unusually smart and apply yourself you'll have a fairly good idea of it after six months of study and rehearsal.

IRENE

A mind reader! Yes—you're quite right. I shall be able to do that very well!

(AUGUSTE *enters from the bar with a bottle of champagne. He refills their glasses, then refills* HARRY'S *glass, gives* HARRY *the bottle and goes back in to the bar.*)

HARRY

And, another thing, if you're going to qualify

for this act with me, you've got to lay off liquor. I mean, after we finish this. It's a well-known fact that booze and science don't mix. (*He has another drink.* IRENE *is as one in a trance.*)

IRENE

I don't think I shall use my own name. No— Americans would mispronounce it horribly. No, I shall call myself—Namoura . . . Namoura the Great—assisted by Harry Van.

HARRY

You've got nice billing there.

IRENE

I shall wear a black velvet dress—very plain— My skin, ivory white. I must have something to hold. One white flower. No! A little white prayer book. That's it. A little white . . . (*The warning siren is heard.*) What's that?

HARRY

Sounds like a fire. (*The* CAPTAIN *and* MAJOR *burst out of the bar and rush to the big window, talking excitedly in Italian and pointing to the northwestern sky. The siren shrieks continue. The* MAJOR *then rushes out, the* CAPTAIN *about to follow him.*) What's up, Captain?

CAPTAIN

French aeroplanes. It is reprisal for last night. They are coming to destroy our base here.

HARRY

I see.

CAPTAIN

They have no reason to attack this hotel. But —there may easily be accidents. I advise the cellar.

(AUGUSTE *rushes in from the bar,* PITTALUGA *from the lobby. The latter orders* AUGUSTE *to lower the Venetian blinds.*)

IRENE

Oh, no, Captain. We must stay here and watch the spectacle.

CAPTAIN

I entreat you not to be reckless, Madame. I have enough on my conscience now, without adding to it your innocent life!

IRENE

Don't worry, Captain. Death and I are old friends.

CAPTAIN

God be with you, Madame.

(*He goes out.* HARRY *and* IRENE *empty their glasses.* HARRY *refills them. Airplane motors are heard, increasing. Then the sound of machine guns.*)

(*Bombs are heard bursting at some distance.* AUGUSTE *and* PITTALUGA *go.*)

IRENE

Those are bombs.

HARRY

I guess so.

IRENE

We're in the war, Harry.

HARRY

What do you think we ought to do about it? Go out and say "Boo"?

IRENE

Let them be idiotic if they wish. We are sane. Why don't you try singing something?

HARRY

The voice don't feel appropriate. Too bad we haven't got Chaliapin here. (*She laughs.*) You know, babe—you look better blonde.

IRENE

Thank you.
(PITTALUGA *runs in.*)

PITTALUGA

The French beasts are bombing us! Every one goes into the cellar.

HARRY

Thanks very much, Signor.

PITTALUGA

You have been warned! (*He rushes out.*)

IRENE

Ridiculous! Here we are, on top of the world—
and he asks us to go down into the cellar. . . . Do
you want to go into the cellar?

HARRY

Do you?

IRENE

No. If a bomb hits, it will be worse in the cellar.
(*He holds her close to him. She kisses him.*) I love
you, Harry.

HARRY

You do, eh!

IRENE

Ever since that night—in the Governor Bryan
Hotel—I've loved you. Because I knew that you
have a heart that I can trust. And that whatever
I would say to you, I would never—*never* be mis-
understood.

HARRY

That's right, babe. I told you I had you tagged,
right from the beginning.

IRENE

And you adore me, don't you, darling?

HARRY

No! Now lay off——

IRENE

No—of course not—you mustn't admit it!

HARRY

Will you please stop pawing me?
(*She laughs and lets go of him.*)
(*HARRY pours more champagne, as she crosses
to the window, opens the slats of the blinds, and
looks out. There is now great noise of planes,
machine guns and bombs.*)

IRENE

Oh, you must see this! It's superb! (*He crosses
to the window with his glass and looks out. The
light on the stage is growing dimmer, but a weird
light comes from the window. The scream of many
gas bombs is heard.*) It's positively Wagnerian—
isn't it?

HARRY

It looks to me exactly like "Hell's Angels." Did
you ever see that picture, babe?

IRENE

No. I don't care for films.

HARRY

I *do.* I love 'em—every one of them. (*He is
dragging her to the piano—a comparatively safe
retreat.*) Did you know I used to play the piano
in picture theatres? Oh, sure—I know all the
music there is.

(*They are now at the piano—HARRY sitting,
IRENE standing close by him. She is looking
toward the window. He starts to accompany the*

air-raid with the "Ride of the Walkyries." *There is a loud explosion.*)

IRENE

Harry . . .

HARRY

Yes, babe?

IRENE

Harry—do you realize that the whole world has gone to war? The *whole world!*

HARRY

I realize it. But don't ask me why. Because I've stopped trying to figure it out.

IRENE

I know why it is. It's just for the purpose of killing *us* . . . you and me. (*There is another loud explosion.* HARRY *stops playing.*) Because we are the little people—and for us the deadliest weapons are the most merciful. . . .

(*Another loud explosion.* HARRY *drinks.*)

HARRY

They're getting closer.

IRENE

Play some more. (*He resumes the* "Walkyrie.") Harry—do you know any hymns?

HARRY

What?

IRENE

Do you know any hymns?

HARRY

Certainly. (*He starts to play* "Onward, Christian Soldiers" *in furious jazz time, working in strains of* "Dixie." *There is another fearful crash, shattering the pane of the big window. He drags her down beside him at the piano.* HARRY *resumes* "Onward, Christian Soldiers" *in a slow, solemn tempo.*)

HARRY (*sings*)

Onward, Christian Soldiers——
(IRENE *joins the loud singing.*)

BOTH (*singing*)

Marching as to war—
With the Cross of Jesus
Going on before. . . .
(*The din is now terrific. Demolition—bombs, gas-bombs, airplanes, shrapnel, machine guns.*)

CURTAIN

POSTSCRIPT

During the past two weeks (this is March 16, 1936) the Italians have made a great offensive in Ethiopia; there has been an outburst of assassination and hara kiri by Fascists in Japan; the British Foreign Secretary, Mr. Eden, has said in the House of Commons that the current situation is "dreadfully similar to 1914"; a mutual assistance treaty has been ratified between republican France and Soviet Russia, and the German army has occupied the Rhineland, thereby shattering all that remained of the treaties of Versailles and Locarno.

What will happen before this play reaches print or a New York audience, I do not know. But let me express here the conviction that those who shrug and say, "War is inevitable," are false prophets. I believe that the world is populated largely by decent people, and decent people don't want war. Nor do they make war. They fight and die, to be sure—but that is because they have been deluded by their exploiters, who are members of the indecent minority.

Of course, this delusion may still go on. If decent people will continue to be intoxicated by the synthetic spirit of patriotism, pumped into them by megalomaniac leaders, and will continue to have faith in the "security" provided by those lethal weapons sold to them by the armaments industry, then war *is* inevitable; and the world will soon resolve itself into the semblance of an ant hill, governed by commissars who owe their power to the profundity of their contempt for the individual members of their species.

But I don't believe this will be so. I believe that a sufficient number of people are aware of the persistent validity of the Sermon on the Mount, and they remember that, between 1914 and 1918, twelve million men died in violence to make safe for democracy the world which we see about us today. That awareness and remembrance can be strong enough to resist the forces which would drive us back into the confusion and the darkness and the filth of No Man's Land.

The megalomaniac, to live, must inspire excitement, fear and awe. If, instead, he is greeted with calmness, courage and ridicule, he becomes a figure of supreme insignificance. A display of the three latter qualities by England, France, the Soviet Union, and the United States will defeat Fascism in Germany, Italy, and Japan, and will remove the threat of war which is Fascism's last gesture of self-justification.

By refusing to imitate the Fascists in their policies of heavily fortified isolation, their hysterical self-worship and psychopathic hatred of others, we may achieve the enjoyment of peaceful life on earth, rather than degraded death in the cellar.

R. E. S.